CHRIST IN ALL THE SCRIPTURES

READING AND PRAYING THROUGH
THE BIBLE IN A YEAR

WRITTEN BY
Eddie Mercado
Tyler Moser
Chris Smith
Corum Hughes

$20.00
ISBN 979-8-218-37993-3
52000>

9 798218 379933

CONCEPT BY
Charles Morris
Tamara Chamberlain

BOOK LAYOUT AND DESIGN
Hilary Alvarado

PRINTED IN
Grand Rapids, Michigan by J.D. Gordon L.L.C.

HAVEN MINISTRIES
PO Box 79997
Riverside, CA 92513

HAVEN CANADA
P.O. Box 19099
Delta, BC V4L 2P8

ISBN: 979-8-218-37993-3
Copyright © 2024 Haven Ministries, Edition 1.2.

CHRIST IN ALL
THE SCRIPTURES

Read and Pray Through

The Bible in a Year

WRITTEN BY

Eddie Mercado

Tyler Moser

Chris Smith

Corum Hughes

EDITED BY

Kathy Daane

Table of Contents

OLD TESTAMENT

NEW TESTAMENT

Introduction

Have you ever read a passage of Scripture and thought, "What exactly does this mean, and what am I supposed to get out of it?" If you have, you're not alone. Some parts of God's Word are easy to understand, while others require more study. One of the first and most important things we have to do is understand that the Bible is one story, and it points to One Person.

In Luke 24 we read the account of two disciples of Christ traveling to a town called Emmaus. It was the same Sunday when Jesus rose from the dead. They were joined by a stranger ... or so they thought Him to be. When asked what they were talking about, they told Him about this Jesus whom they hoped would be the Messiah, how He was killed on a cross, and how some of the believing women reported that His tomb was empty.

But then something happened they didn't expect.

This stranger began to teach: "*He said to them, 'How foolish you are, and how slow to believe all that the prophets have spoken! Did not the Christ have to suffer these things and then enter his glory?' And beginning with Moses and all the Prophets, he explained to them what was said in all the Scriptures concerning himself*" (24:25–27). This was actually the risen Christ, hidden from their eyes, saying that all of God's Word points to Him.

At Haven Ministries we love to share the great story that's all about Jesus. It's easy to say, but sometimes it's difficult to see exactly how the entire Bible points to Christ. Will you join us as we go through the Scriptures book by book? Along the way, we'll see even more of our Great Savior. And as with those two disciples on the road to Emmaus, Jesus will often show up where we least expect Him.

HOW TO USE THIS BOOK

Over the next 365 days, you will journey through the entire Bible. This book is designed not only to help you find Jesus in the text, but also to pray to Jesus throughout your journey into God's Word. This is done in three ways:

1. DAILY READINGS

Each day you will read through 2-4 chapters of the Bible at a time. If you find yourself missing a day or two, just pick up where you left off. Move at the pace you are comfortable with, and don't feel pressure to skip ahead. Certainly there is great reason to celebrate reading the entire Bible in one year, but opening your heart and mind for the Holy Spirit to draw you nearer to Jesus is far greater. This also will allow you to better meditate through weekly prayers on what you've read.

2. WEEKLY PRAYERS

Each week, this book will provide you with a new prayer that is drawn from the corresponding week's Scripture readings. Pray it. Meditate on it. Let it grow within you. By having you repeat one prayer every day over a section of readings, it is our hope that the Spirit behind each verse will become more real to you, and that you will draw nearer to the Father through Jesus in your daily life. Though you will pray the same words each day for a week, we are confident they will hold new meaning by day seven.

3. BOOK INTRODUCTIONS

Before you begin each new book of the Bible, you will be presented with a book overview that includes helpful insights and details about the book and how it points to Christ. This valuable background information will help you better understand the reading ahead. But, don't worry! We know you'll be doing a lot of reading over the next 12 months, so while they are chock-full of Christ-focused content, we've kept these short.

We hope you will find this to be a valuable reading and prayer guide through Scripture. However, as you embark on this journey to read through the entire Bible, our utmost prayer is that you come away with Jesus.

OLD TESTAMENT

Genesis

"Once upon a time."

We've all heard these familiar words. They
tell us that a story is just beginning — the stage
is being set. After all, every good story begins
somewhere. And the great story that's all about
Jesus is no different. Actually, there is one big
difference: this story starts at the beginning of time.
That's when God created the heavens and the earth.
Maybe we don't think about that enough.

Everything we have ever seen, touched,
smelled, heard, and tasted is the result of God
creating all things out of nothing. And because
He created it all, He also owns it all. He is the
King above all kings. This Creator King made the
first man and woman. Think about it: God spoke

everything into existence, except for humankind. The Lord stooped down and hand-crafted the first human couple. He gave them everything they needed, but He also gave them commands.

We know what happened, of course. The serpent deceived Eve, she ate, and she gave the fruit to Adam. He ate, too. That's where it all went wrong. Every human being who has been born since then is a sinner, with the exception of Jesus. And speaking of Him, how do we see Christ in Genesis? Well, He shows up at the beginning. We read the first promise of the gospel in Genesis 3:15. Speaking to the serpent (who is the devil), the Lord said, "*I will put enmity between you and the woman, and between your offspring and hers; he will crush your head, and you will strike his heel.*"

From the start our God was gracious to sinners (and Genesis has no shortage of them!). The first 11 chapters fly through generation after generation. Century after century passes into the rearview mirror. And then, in chapter 12, it slows to a snail's pace. Why? Because the main characters are finally here. Genesis is the story of how the Lord set apart a people for Himself. He promised that One Seed of the woman would come. Then He revealed Himself to one man: Abram. Chapters 12-

50 encompass only four generations. God promises all of them that He will be gracious to them, and that through their family line the One promised in Genesis 3:15 will come.

The book ends with the descendants of Abraham shepherding sheep in Egypt, which makes sense because this book was written to the Exodus generation of Israelites. It was a prologue, telling them how, instead of the so-called gods and goddesses of Egypt, the Lord made and rules over everything. It tells of how God had set them and their ancestors apart for Himself, and how they eventually reached the Promised Land.

Once upon a time...

WEEK 1

GENESIS 1 – 25

Our Great Father in heaven, we praise You for Your wonderful power over all things. You spoke and created everything out of nothing. You sustain all things. If You withdrew Your upholding hand, all of creation would fade into nothingness. But beyond this, we also see Your goodness and love to us. You responded with grace and mercy when Adam and Eve sinned in the Garden of Eden. You promised a Seed who would come and redeem us, defeating Satan in the process. You are the promise-keeping God, and we know that You have kept Your Word. Jesus Christ lived and died and rose again for us, and everyone on earth has been blessed in Him. We read about Your faithfulness to Abraham and Isaac, and we know You will remain faithful to us, too. May your name be praised, Father, Son, and Holy Spirit!

AMEN.

☐ *Day 1:* Genesis 1–4
☐ *Day 2:* Genesis 5–8
☐ *Day 3:* Genesis 9–12
☐ *Day 4:* Genesis 13–17
☐ *Day 5:* Genesis 18–20
☐ *Day 6:* Genesis 21–23
☐ *Day 7:* Genesis 24–25

WEEK 2

GENESIS 26 – 46

Oh, Lord, You are the One who provides for Your people.
We know that every good gift, even every breath we take,
comes to us from Your loving hand. We recognize that we
often sin in the same ways that our ancestors did, just as
Isaac failed in the same way his father Abraham failed. But
You don't deal with us according to what our sin deserves.
Truly You are full of grace and mercy for sinners such as
us! We confess our sins to You and throw ourselves on
the mercy and grace we find in Christ. We read how good
You are in raising up Joseph who was treated so harshly.
We know this is a picture of our Lord Jesus, who was
mistreated — the Sinless One slaughtered in the place of
sinners. Yet you raised Him up, not only out of the grave,
but to sit at Your right hand even now. We come to You in
prayer, knowing that we don't deserve to be heard because
of who we are or what we have done, but only because we
come in Christ's precious and powerful name.

AMEN.

☐ *Day 8:* Genesis 26–28
☐ *Day 9:* Genesis 29–31
☐ *Day 10:* Genesis 32–35
☐ *Day 11:* Genesis 36–38
☐ *Day 12:* Genesis 39–41
☐ *Day 13:* Genesis 42–43
☐ *Day 14:* Genesis 44–46

Exodus

Genesis ended on a high note. Even though Jacob died, the Lord used Joseph to save his family. The people of God were now safe and successful within the borders of Egypt, one of the superpowers of the day. God was really fulfilling His promises to Abraham, Isaac, and Jacob, wasn't He? But every story has its ups and downs. And the great story that's all about Jesus is no different. *"Then a new king, who did not know about Joseph, came to power in Egypt"* (1:8). The Israelites became slaves in Egypt. Would God keep the promises He made to Abraham, Isaac, and Jacob? Who was really in charge here, Pharaoh or the Lord? Would God redeem a sinful people? Exodus answers these questions, and it does so by showing that the Lord is not only *great*, He is also *good*. As Yahweh Himself says, "*They will know that I am the LORD their God, who brought them out of Egypt so that I might dwell among them. I am the LORD their God*" (29:46). He delivered them *from* oppression and bondage, *into* His own presence.

But we're getting ahead of ourselves. Before God could dwell among His people, He had to deliver them. So the Lord went to war. First He chose and sent His ambassador, Moses, with a message to let God's people go. When Pharaoh didn't listen, the One True God declared holy war against the Egyptian false gods. Each of the plagues He sent was an attack on one of the Egyptian idols. It quickly became clear that Yahweh alone is God. Pharaoh and his false gods were powerless to stop Him. So Pharaoh let the people go. Finally, after four centuries, the people of God were free again! But then Pharaoh had a change of heart. God used the Red Sea to deliver His people and to bring judgment on their enemies.

That's the first part of the book of Exodus — God easily delivering His people from one of the most powerful rulers of the day. Then we come to the second part of the book, God living with these sinful complainers without killing them. He brought them to Mount Sinai and gave them the Ten Commandments. But as Moses was still hearing from the Lord, the people were at the base of the mountain creating an idol. It was like committing adultery on the wedding night.

They had no more physical chains, but the spiritual chains of sin remained. God had redeemed them outwardly, yet they needed to be redeemed spiritually. And while they waited for the Seed of the woman and the Offspring of Abraham to come, they needed to be kept separate from God. He would dwell in their midst, but there must be barriers between a holy God and His sinful people. Specifically, there had to be curtains. The Lord gave Moses instructions for the tabernacle where Israel's King would put His special presence, keeping the sinful people from coming too close.

Much of the rest of the Old Testament asks this question: "Who can draw near to God?" We will find that the answer is Jesus, and through Him we also have access to our Father. The curtain has been torn from top to bottom. A new, better Moses has led us through the great Exodus. Destination: the New Heavens and Earth.

WEEK 3

GENESIS 47–EXODUS 20

Oh, great and powerful God, nothing ever catches You by surprise. You used the cruel treatment of Joseph by his brothers to save them and the world. As Joseph said, what man intended for evil, You intended for good. Though a famine threatened Your promise made to Abraham, You preserved humanity so that Your saving purposes would continue. Though Pharaoh planned to destroy the Israelites, You used an Israelite growing up in Pharaoh's house to set Your people free! From famines, to persecution, even to the death of Your Son, Jesus Christ, You've used these dark moments for Your glory and the deliverance of Your people. Remind us of this truth when we're in times of suffering. We pray this in Jesus' name.

AMEN.

☐ *Day 15:* Genesis 47–50
☐ *Day 16:* Exodus 1–4
☐ *Day 17:* Exodus 5–7
☐ *Day 18:* Exodus 8–10
☐ *Day 19:* Exodus 11–13
☐ *Day 20:* Exodus 14–16
☐ *Day 21:* Exodus 17–20

WEEK 4

EXODUS 21–LEVITICUS 4

Father, we confess that it can be hard reading through Your law. As we read chapter after chapter of various laws, we struggle to see the relevance in our lives. Yet they are important because they reveal Your character. You are a holy God who desires a holy people. You called Israel to holiness. They were to be set apart for You in every aspect of their lives. But they quickly deserted their call to be holy. Instead of worshiping You, they made a golden calf. We can be quick to judge, but we realize we are no different. With one hand we honor You, but with the other we push You away. Like the Israelites, we are in need of forgiveness. Thank you for Jesus, the Mediator greater than Moses, and the One who makes us holy.

AMEN.

☐ *Day 22:* Exodus 21–23
☐ *Day 23:* Exodus 24–27
☐ *Day 24:* Exodus 28–30
☐ *Day 25:* Exodus 31–34
☐ *Day 26:* Exodus 35–37
☐ *Day 27:* Exodus 38–40
☐ *Day 28:* Leviticus 1–4

Leviticus

Leviticus is where many plans to read through the
Bible in a year come to die. It just seems so alien to
us, doesn't it? Priests, sacrifices, ritual cleanliness and
impurity. What does this have to do with us? More
importantly, what does this have to do with Jesus? The
answer might surprise us: Christ's ministry and our
redemption wouldn't make sense without this book.
Really, Leviticus reminds us that God is holy and we are
sinful. We cannot just waltz into the Lord's presence,
presuming on Him. No, we have to be invited, and we
have to come on His terms. How else could sinners like
us approach this God who is a consuming fire?

Yahweh saved the Israelites from Egypt. But if
they were going to live in His presence in His land, then
they would have to follow His rules. They would have to

be holy. And they would have to do what God required when they *weren't* holy, which happened quite often. Once again, the concept of "separations" is important.

Perhaps thinking about separations is the best way to read and interpret law passages. Certain things were set apart for God in a special way, and these things were "sacred." Whatever was not set apart for God in this special way was "common." There was nothing necessarily wrong with the common things; they just had a different relationship to God than the sacred things. Israel was sacred and the other nations were common because only the children of Abraham, Isaac, and Jacob had a covenant relationship with God at this time in history. As His sacred people, they must obey Him in holiness.

But then there's the other distinction we find all over Leviticus: the difference between "pure" and "impure." Ritual impurity came from a variety of things in an Israelite's day-to-day life. It was not necessarily a sin to be ritually impure, but it was a sin to approach sacred things (like the tabernacle) while impure. Impurity was contagious, but purity was not. If God's people were planning to come into His presence, they were to keep away from other impure people or objects. The process for returning to purity often included washing, waiting, and sometimes offering sacrifices.

Israel failed to keep the law, but God included built-in failsafes: sacrifices. The burnt offering was completely consumed by the fire of the altar, signifying that believers must be fully committed to the Lord. Grain offerings acknowledged that God provided everything His people needed. Fellowship offerings indicated the importance of a deep relationship with the Creator and Redeemer. Sin and guilt offerings showed the effects of sin and the necessity of being brought back into a close relationship with God after the sinner broke His law and failed to be holy.

How does Jesus fit into all of this? A holy God can dwell with His sinful, impure people only if full satisfaction and reconciliation have been made between them. Jesus is the perfect sacrifice, and He is our High Priest who is interceding for us in heaven. Because of Christ — God in human flesh — we can know that God will always dwell in our midst in a way much more intimate and final than He did in the tabernacle.

In Christ we are counted as pure and holy — God has given us all we need to safely come into His presence. Through Him we are *"a chosen people, a royal priesthood, a holy nation, God's special possession, that [we] may declare the praises of him who called [us] out of darkness into his wonderful light"* (1 Peter 2:9). The way is open!

WEEK 5

LEVITICUS 5–23

God, You are holy, holy, holy. The offerings that You required of Israel show that You cannot be in the presence of sin. If we want to approach Your presence, we must be cleansed by the blood of a sacrifice. The Day of Atonement speaks of two goats; one was sacrificed as an offering, and the other was driven out into the wilderness, carrying the sins of Israel with it. Jesus, we know You are both the sacrificial offering who paid for our sins, and the scapegoat who was driven out of God's presence and into the wilderness. You died on a cross so that we might live. You cried, "Father, why have you forsaken me?" so that we would be welcomed in. What amazing love! We praise You, Father, that despite our sinfulness and because of Your kindness and mercy, You made a way to bring us into Your presence.

AMEN.

Numbers

The theme of Numbers is exactly what the book's title indicates: math. But don't tune out! God had been with Abraham's descendants, the Israelites. He had watched over them, rescuing them from Egypt. In fact, the book of Exodus tells us that even while they were enslaved, they were multiplying! So the book of Numbers tells us how many of them there were. Two censuses were taken, one recorded in chapter 6 and the other in chapter 26.

There's a lot more going on in this book than just counting, however. We see the Israelites on their way to Canaan, the Promised Land. And — wouldn't you know it? — they complained and disobeyed. Even though they had seen the Lord's miracles in Egypt, sometimes they still doubted and even rebelled, especially when they came to the border of the Promised Land. Twelve spies went in, but ten of them brought back a terrifying report of giants living in fortified cities there. Only Joshua and Caleb were sure that God could win the victory for them. The people listened to the ten doubters and rebelled against God one time too many. The Lord refused to let any Israelite 20 years or older into the Promised Land, with the exception of Joshua and Caleb, who believed. Even Moses disobeyed and was denied entrance.

Though God had to discipline His unbelieving and disobedient people, He remained committed to His promises to Abraham, Isaac, and Jacob. He would still bring the next generation into the Promised Land. He would give them Canaan. But how would He do this? The book of Numbers never reveals the specifics. We are left with the knowledge that there's a Promised Land, that God's people are sinful, and that He's going to lead them to this place despite their sin.

That sounds familiar to us, doesn't it? We have an even better Promised Land: the New Heavens and Earth. But we're just as sinful as the ancient Israelites were. We can't earn this land any more than they could earn Canaan. Can the Lord be righteous and just and still bless us, His sinful and disobedient people? We all sin — every one of us. Jesus alone obeyed perfectly in the place of His people. He is the great Israel, the Servant we needed. He also paid the price for all of our disobedience, sin, doubt, and murmurings. And that's how we enter the ultimate Promised Land. That's how we come into the rest God has presented to us. Jesus is a better Israel. He's a better Moses. He's the Savior we need. And He leads us into His Land. Is that where you're going?

WEEK 6

LEVITICUS 24–NUMBERS 10

Oh, Lord, Your presence is our greatest blessing. At times we feel overwhelmed like the Israelites did when they settled near Mount Sinai. They heard Your will from Moses and tried to keep the purity laws while wandering in the desert. It may have been tempting to grow cynical. But You were using this to prepare them for a journey that would include battle and rebellion. They would need preparation and purity, but they also would need Your presence. Your presence is required for our journey today, too. Remind us that You will bless us and keep us, and that You will shine Your face upon us and be gracious to us. The Israelites knew You were with them when the cloud descended on the tabernacle. We know You are with us by Your Spirit which now dwells within us.

AMEN.

☐ *Day 36:* Leviticus 24–25
☐ *Day 37:* Leviticus 26–27
☐ *Day 38:* Numbers 1–2
☐ *Day 39:* Numbers 3–4
☐ *Day 40:* Numbers 5–6
☐ *Day 41:* Numbers 7
☐ *Day 42:* Numbers 8–10

WEEK 7

NUMBERS 11–29

Great God and King, we confess that we are so often like the Israelites. You showed us Your kindness by providing salvation in Christ Jesus, and yet we are prone to wander. We're like the Israelites who lacked faith in Your promise to bring them into the Promised Land. Forgive us. Help us. May Your Holy Spirit give us the strength to walk by faith and not by sight. Though we see giants in our midst, You have promised to be with us. To keep Your promise, You used the false prophet Balaam to bless the people of Israel. Through Balaam You even pointed Israel forward to the Messiah, Jesus Christ, who would rule over all the nations. Though Israel was faithless throughout the journey, You were faithful. You are the same God today that You were then. Thank You for Your faithfulness.

AMEN.

Deuteronomy

Here we go again! Nearly all of the Israelites from the generation that had rebelled against God in the book of Numbers were dead and gone. Their children had grown up and had families of their own. This was it! The people of Israel were finally ready to enter the Promised Land after wandering in the wilderness for 40 years. There it was, just on the other side of the Jordan River, ready to be entered.

But first, the Israelites had to hear God's law again. That's what "Deuteronomy" means; it's Latin for "Second Law." Not that this was a different law than the one God had given to Israel decades before. No, this was the same law given a second time to a new generation. The Lord was reminding them that this was His Land, and they had to be holy and obey

Him or He would evict them. He had saved them
from slavery in Egypt; now they were compelled to be
grateful and obedient. That's why so much of what we
read in this book seems familiar: God was reiterating
the important things to His forgetful people.

That doesn't mean there's nothing new in
Deuteronomy. Far from it! The biggest change had to
do with leadership. Moses was not allowed to enter
the Promised Land. He had also rebelled against
God. So as he gave these final instructions to Israel,
he knew he wouldn't be going with them. Instead, he
would hand off the baton to Joshua. But first, Moses
rehearsed what the Lord had graciously done for His
people. He urged them to remain faithful in the land
and to remember what would happen if they obeyed
or disobeyed.

That's really the key here. Deuteronomy
reminds us that God is gracious and merciful, but also
holy and just. If there's going to be a relationship of
blessing between God and humanity, then humanity
has to obey. But Israel didn't obey. And neither
do we. In fact, ever since Adam and Eve fell in the
Garden, no human has obeyed, except for One. Jesus
Christ did what we should do. What Israel should've
done. What Adam failed to do. Jesus obeyed perfectly
in the place of His people, so that we don't have

to look to our own law-keeping in order to earn or keep our salvation. Our Savior has already earned it for us, and He surely will keep it! Our relationship with God is as certain as His Son's spotless and complete obedience. Jesus is the Mediator who obeyed perfectly, and unlike Moses, He takes us into the ultimate Promised Land. Our Leader is also our Law-Keeper. How can we not gratefully obey such a gracious Savior?

WEEK 8

NUMBERS 30–DEUTERONOMY 15

Heavenly Father, You know us well. You know that we are forgetful, which is why You used Moses to remind Israel (and us!) of who You are and what You have done. Yes, there was judgment involved due to Israel's rebellion, but You were still with them. You are still with us, despite our failures. What a source of comfort that is! Just as You watched over the Israelites in their wilderness journey, so You watch over us in our journey. You protect us from our enemies. You provide nourishment for us. You have revealed Your will to us through Your Word so that we may know how to love You with all our heart, soul, and strength. Remind us that we are dependent only on You. We need You, God. Remain with us. In Jesus' name,

AMEN.

☐ *Day 50:* Numbers 30–32
☐ *Day 51:* Numbers 33–36
☐ *Day 52:* Deuteronomy 1–2
☐ *Day 53:* Deuteronomy 3–4
☐ *Day 54:* Deuteronomy 5–8
☐ *Day 55:* Deuteronomy 9–11
☐ *Day 56:* Deuteronomy 12–15

WEEK 9

DEUTERONOMY 16–34

Father, You abound in wisdom. We know that You established laws that would preserve peace, instruct Your people how to govern their land, and teach Your people that they could not pay for their own sins. You also used the covenant renewal ceremony to show Israel that they were not able to perfectly keep Your covenant. The covenant must be kept by another. In Your infinite wisdom, You used all these signs to point to Jesus Christ. Thank You for providing the spotless sacrifice and covenant keeper that Israel needed, and yes, the One that we need. Thank You for sending Your Son to be our Savior.

AMEN.

Joshua

No pressure. Joshua was just following in the
footsteps of Moses himself ... that's all! The great
leader was dead, and now Joshua had been chosen
by God as the one to take Israel into the Promised
Land. It was time for the conquest. But first,
the Lord had to remind Joshua to be strong and
courageous. The God of all the Universe would be
with him. And what a well-timed reminder this was.
The Israelites crossed the Jordan River, which God
parted in the same way that He parted the waters of
the Red Sea in Exodus. So far so good, right?

    That's when God called a timeout. His
people were ready to go, but before they began their
first battle at Jericho, they circumcised the males
and celebrated the Passover. Although they were far

from perfect, they showed they were at least more committed to Yahweh than their parents had been. During this time, Joshua received an unexpected visit from Someone who came to him under the name *"the commander of the army of the Lord."* And He didn't kill Joshua. Yes, that's a big deal. An angelic figure with a drawn sword, standing at the eastern border of God's land would harken back to Genesis 3 where the cherubim and flaming sword kept Adam and Eve away from Eden. Well, Joshua and the Israelites weren't driven away; God allowed His people to enter.

Though the Israelites were allowed in, a quick and easy campaign was not in the Lord's plans for them. They had ups and downs, depending on their obedience or disobedience. But ultimately their hope was certain, because their God and Redeemer was going before them.

This was far from a normal war. Just think about the Battle of Jericho: not exactly sound military strategy, was it? Yet God promised that He would give victory to His people. In fact, Joshua's name means "God saves." The Lord used this deliverer to lead His people to their promised rest. After many battles, they started divvying up the property and settled down in cities and villages. God used Joshua to give His people rest.

Well ... mostly. By the time Joshua died, the Israelites were in possession of a large part of Canaan, but many Canaanites still remained in the land. The work was not yet done. After Joshua's death, the people needed another leader like him, one who would courageously lead them in righteousness and faithfulness and deliver them from their enemies. Yahweh had worked through Joshua, leading His people into the Promised Land and giving them victory and rest. But this Joshua was just a preview of Someone else. The name "Jesus" is a Greek version of the Hebrew name "Joshua." And He's the Ultimate Savior, the perfectly obedient One who leads His people not into temporary rest in Canaan, but into everlasting rest in the New Heavens and Earth. The One who conquered sin and death is our Joshua. Trust Him. Follow Him. And He will give you rest.

WEEK 10

JOSHUA 1–22

God, if we are honest, we must admit that times of transition can be difficult for us. We get scared of the unknown and anxious about change. But Lord, You never change. Knowing all things, You prepared the right individual to lead Israel after Moses died. Knowing the hearts of Your people, You gave Joshua a word of encouragement: be strong and courageous. We need this word, God. In the midst of the uncertainties of this life, remind us to be strong and courageous, not because we are strong, but because You are strong. You are the God who brought Israel across the Jordan. You are the God who caused Jericho to fall. You are the God who made the sun stand still. Nothing is impossible for You! Whenever we approach seasons filled with unknowns, help us to look back to the Ebenezer stones which testify to Your faithfulness. In Jesus' name,

AMEN.

Judges

Joshua was dead. The man who had led Israel in the conquest gave his final address to the people and dismissed them. That's the last they saw of him. Just like with Moses' death years before, the people of God were in the middle of a big transition. But instead of another Joshua taking over, there was a leadership void. God didn't choose an individual as a replacement. Instead, the job of obeying the Lord and finishing the conquest of the Promised Land fell on all of the people of Israel. And the people weren't up to the task. They quickly began to sin against their Lord, worshiping other gods and doing things their own way. Israel was in Canaan, and they were in danger of becoming just like the Canaanites they were supposed to conquer. So God responded by reminding them how hard life would be without Him.

This was the beginning of what is often called the "Judges Cycle." The people of Israel would be faithless and sin against God, God would send a foreign nation to oppress them, Israel would repent of their sin and cry out to God for deliverance, God would graciously send a deliverer (known as a "judge"), and things would be better while the judge was alive. But once the judge was gone, the cycle would start again.

Throughout the book, we read of the judges growing worse and worse. Eventually, we come to Samson, a man who never fought to deliver the people and only fought for himself. The Philistines still oppressed God's people even after his death; there was no deliverance at the end of the book. Judges ends with these sobering words: "*In those days Israel had no king; everyone did as they saw fit.*" The problems kept multiplying, but what was the answer? What did Israel need? A king who would lead them in righteousness and faithfulness, someone who would fill the void left by Joshua's death. Where could such a king be found? The short-term answer was David.

But we need a long-term answer, Someone even better than David. And that's exactly what we get in Jesus Christ, the King of kings. God has graciously provided redemption and deliverance for us. We have a King! He has fought and won for us. Let's live like it.

WEEK 11

JOSHUA 23–JUDGES 16

Oh, Lord, God of Israel, as we read of Joshua giving the most important ultimatum in Israel's history, we know we are given this ultimatum as well. Whom will we serve — the gods of this world, or the living and true God? Lord, we cling to You! In You, eternal life is found. But we know following You is not easy. Our spiritual journey is marked by bumps and stops, valleys and long desert highways. This journey can be difficult. Please help us avoid the terrible detours that Israel took during the time of the Judges. Within 40 years, they had forgotten their covenant with You. God, keep us from falling into that same trap. Help us remain faithful to Your Word. Holy Spirit, grant us strength to fight against the temptation. We pray this in Jesus' name,

AMEN.

☐ *Day 71:* Joshua 23–24
☐ *Day 72:* Judges 1–3
☐ *Day 73:* Judges 4–5
☐ *Day 74:* Judges 6–8
☐ *Day 75:* Judges 9–10
☐ *Day 76:* Judges 11–13
☐ *Day 77:* Judges 14–16

Ruth

The time of the judges was one of the low points in Israel's history. Disobedience and judgment were everywhere. The book of Ruth focuses on one family during this time.

A man named Elimelech had a wife named Naomi and two sons named Mahlon and Chilion. At first glance, that may not sound significant to us. But here's that sentence again with the Hebrew names translated into English: A man named *My God Is King* had a wife named *Pleasant* and two sons named *Sickness* and *Annihilation*. Now that puts a different spin on things, doesn't it? The story begins in Bethlehem, the *House of Bread*. But there was no food in this city. What happened to the land flowing with milk and honey? God's judgment had come upon it. Israel had sinned, and Yahweh essentially turned off the water to His land.

So this family decided to do what you might call a reverse Exodus. They left the Promised Land and went to unbelieving gentile territory in search of the good life. In other words, the man whose name meant *My God Is King* lived like his God wasn't really on the throne at all. In the days of the judges, this family chose to do what was right in their own eyes, and judgment followed them. Elimelech died. His sons took Moabite wives, and then their names proved to be very fitting as they died young. Elimelech's family had been reduced to three widows. Moab, the land of food, had become a land of barrenness when it came to life and happiness.

Yet after all of this, Yahweh gave His people food in Bethlehem. The Lord, Israel's covenant keeping God, initiated salvation for His people. He remained faithful. God always works in the darkest moments. Following after the good life in a sinful way left Naomi mourning and bitter. But God worked through this to bring Ruth, the unexpected convert, with her. And the Lord brought Ruth right into the fields of Boaz, a relative. He was a faithful, godly man who went above and beyond the call of duty for the sake of Ruth and Naomi. God worked

through Boaz to deliver these two women who
had nothing to offer. In time, Boaz and Ruth were
married, and the Lord gave them a child to continue
the family line, a line which would eventually
include King David and Jesus Christ Himself. You
see, the Lord was at work, not only providing for
Naomi and Ruth, but also providing for Israel who
needed a king, and for all who call on God's name
needing a Savior.

"*In those days Israel had no king,*" but that
was about to change. Just like He does today, God
remained faithful even in the darkest times. It was
never darker than when Christ hung on the cross.
Yet as in the early chapters of Ruth, God was still
at work. Preserving. Providing. Redeeming. Trust
in your Savior even in the dark times. Boaz is only
a shadow and preview of this Great Redeemer. Are
you trusting Him?

1 & 2 Samuel

After Samson, we have the last two judges of Israel: Eli and Samuel. Neither delivered Israel, although Samuel was more faithful than Eli. The people rebelled against Samuel's judgeship and ultimately against God who raised him up, and they did so by demanding a king. It wasn't their desire for a king that was the problem, for God had indicated as far back as Deuteronomy 17 that this was His plan all along.

The problem was that they wanted a king like all the other nations. Their hearts were not set on a king to lead them in righteousness under the authority of God the Great King. Instead they wanted a king who would replace God as their leader, protector, and provider. God directed Samuel to anoint Saul from the tribe of Benjamin as king over Israel. Initially it seemed that he would do well. He was physically impressive and good-looking, and he defeated the Ammonites shortly after being declared king. Saul would ultimately be rejected by God, however, after a history of disobedience. He was the kind of king Israel wanted, but not the kind they needed.

At this point in the story we meet David, the son of Jesse, from the tribe of Judah. Not as physically impressive as King Saul or even his own elder brothers, David was the one God directed Samuel to anoint as king over His people. Soon after this anointing, we read the story of David and Goliath. David, still very young and years away from actually becoming king of Israel, defeated a giant Philistine and so began to deliver God's people in a way that Saul (as well as Samuel, Eli, and Samson) had not.

Saul soon grew jealous of David and tried on a number of occasions to kill him. David became an outlaw, and so the king after God's own heart was hunted by the king God rejected. Saul died after losing a battle against the Philistines, further cementing the fact that he was rejected by God and had failed to deliver Israel.

There was then a civil war between the tribe of Judah, under the rule of David, and the rest of the tribes of Israel under Ish-bosheth, the son of Saul.

David prevailed and was proclaimed king over all the tribes. He was victorious over the enemies of God's people. Finally, a deliverer had come! The people of Israel were no longer oppressed as David's kingdom grew quite powerful. He became the standard for the type of king Israel needed. Kings would rule God's people until they went into exile hundreds of years later.

The Israelites needed a king somewhat like David but also far greater than him. David sinned horribly when he sexually abused Bathsheba, had her husband Uriah murdered, and lied about the whole thing. God made a covenant with David in 2 Samuel 7 that there would always be one of his descendants on the throne. We see that the promised Seed which had come through Eve, Noah, Shem, Abraham, Isaac, Jacob, and Judah would also now come through David. The list of possible saviors was being narrowed down slowly but surely. God worked through the humble person who trusted in the Lord, not the proud person who trusted in himself. He used Hannah, Samuel, and David, but we're still left waiting for the humble King who would obey perfectly: David's descendant, Jesus Christ.

WEEK 12

JUDGES 17–1 SAMUEL 14

Father, the closing chapters of Judges are hard to read. They are filled with the accounts of heartbreaking sins. In moments like these, we have a hard time figuring out why this is in Scripture. And yet, because You inspired these words, we know there is a reason. In the face of wars and reprehensible acts against the most vulnerable, we are reminded that Your plan of salvation is not yet fulfilled. As we read of sinful judges and priests, we look forward to our great Judge and High Priest, Jesus Christ. The judges and priests of Israel could only provide temporary relief for the people. But Jesus is a Judge who changes hearts, and a Priest who atones for His people's sins. He is our King who defends us. We thank You, Jesus, for what You have done!

AMEN.

☐ *Day 78:* Judges 17–19
☐ *Day 79:* Judges 20–21
☐ *Day 80:* Ruth 1–4
☐ *Day 81:* 1 Samuel 1–3
☐ *Day 82:* 1 Samuel 4–7
☐ *Day 83:* 1 Samuel 8–12
☐ *Day 84:* 1 Samuel 13–14

WEEK 13

1 SAMUEL 15–2 SAMUEL 3

Oh, God, You are the One who appoints all rulers. Israel was given a king, but it did not turn out the way they expected. King Saul wanted to do things his own way. He would go against Your word and justify it, but as You've said, *"To obey is better than sacrifice."* The disappointment of King Saul showed Israel that a greater king was still to come, a king after Your own heart. We see this in young David whom You used to defeat the great giant, Goliath. Though David was being hunted by jealous Saul, You kept him safe. When David had a chance to hunt Saul himself, he resisted and sought to honor You. But David is not the end of the story. The true king of Israel is Your Son, Jesus Christ, who is also the Son of David! Lord Jesus, thank You for being our glorious and spotless King.

AMEN.

☐ *Day 85:* 1 Samuel 15–16
☐ *Day 86:* 1 Samuel 17–18
☐ *Day 87:* 1 Samuel 19–21
☐ *Day 88:* 1 Samuel 22–24
☐ *Day 89:* 1 Samuel 25–27
☐ *Day 90:* 1 Samuel 28–31
☐ *Day 91:* 2 Samuel 1–3

WEEK 14

2 SAMUEL 4–24

Father, You call us to be patient, and to wait on Your promises. It was no different for David who had to wait many years to finally be crowned king. But You fulfilled Your promise. What's more, You made a greater promise: to give him an everlasting kingdom. Would this promise be broken because of David's awful sin against You? Would Your promise to never leave us nor forsake us be broken because we sin against You? No! God, You are merciful and kind. Just as You forgave David of his sins, so You also forgive us of ours. David's sins and our sins are paid by Jesus, who reigns forever and ever. When we sin, help us to look to Jesus. When we run away, bring us back to repentance. In Jesus' name,

AMEN.

1 & 2 Kings

It was the end of an era. David, the king of Israel
and the man after God's own heart, was leaving
the scene. Who would take his place and lead the
Lord's people? After David died, the kingdom
passed to his son, Solomon (after some political
intrigue). During Solomon's reign, the people
of God reached their high point: they had peace,
power, and almost unbelievable prosperity. It was
during Solomon's reign that the temple of God
was built in Jerusalem as a permanent tabernacle.
At the temple's dedication ceremony, the special
presence of God descended in such a powerful
way that the priests were driven out and unable to
perform their priestly duties.

God now dwelt in the midst of His people

on His holy mountain, Zion, in His holy city, Jerusalem. But for all that he accomplished and all the peace and prosperity of the people of God under his rule, Solomon was not the Messiah. He married 1,000 women, and they turned his heart to other gods and goddesses. Once Solomon died, things went downhill quickly. His son, Rehoboam, acted foolishly and the northern ten tribes broke off from Judah and Benjamin to form their own nation with their own kings, the first of whom was Jeroboam. For the rest of their history, the northern kingdom was called *Israel* and the southern kingdom was known as *Judah*.

King Jeroboam was worried that the people of the north would keep going to the temple in Jerusalem in order to participate in the feasts and sacrifices, which might have eventually lead to reunification. Because of this, he built separate temples and erected golden calves for Israel to worship as if they were God. He became the negative standard for the kings of Israel who followed him; often when a northern king was wicked (and they all were!), it would be said of him that he was *"walking in the way of Jeroboam ... making Israel to sin"* (1 Kings 16:19). Israel's kings were the opposite of the kind of king that the people of God needed. In the south the kings were from the line of David, but they were an up-and-down group. Sometimes a king would come along who led Israel to obey, and of him it would be said that he *"did what was right in the eyes of the LORD, as David his father had done"* (1 Kings 15:11). These were the kinds of kings that the people of God needed, but none of them were *the* king who would reign perfectly.

Soon after Israel split into two separate nations, prophets began coming to them. The most famous of the early prophets were Elijah and Elisha. A true prophet sent by God functioned, you might say, as God's lawyer in a lawsuit against His people. Israel had broken the covenant, and the prophets came to call them to repentance and declare the covenant curses if they refused to change course.

But they were unsuccessful in bringing the people to repentance. Eventually, the people of God broke the covenant so egregiously that the ultimate curse of the covenant fell on them: they were sent into exile. The northern kingdom of Israel was destroyed by the Assyrian empire in 722 B.C., and the southern kingdom of Judah was destroyed by the Babylonian empire in 586 B.C. The book of Kings was written to tell the remnant of Judah why they had ended up in exile. But the story ends with mercy! The Babylonian king released Jehoiachin, the last king of Judah, and let him dine at the royal Babylonian table. Judgment was not the last word; there was still grace to be found. God wasn't done with humanity. But before the situation could be fixed, the Son of God Himself would have to go into exile and suffer the penalty for the sins of His people.

WEEK 15

1 KINGS 1–18

Oh, God and King of Israel, You are wiser than all kings. Solomon knew this (which is why when You offered to give him whatever he asked, Solomon asked You for wisdom). We admit that we need wisdom! So often we find ourselves making rash decisions, acting instead of taking time to pray and read Your Word. Lord, help us to seek Your will. Your wisdom was revealed with the temple as You assured Israel of Your presence among them and displayed Your worldwide plan of redemption. Along with Solomon, we pray for the nations. Please hear the prayers of those who call upon You. Let the gospel move forward so that people from every tribe, tongue, and nation will know Your name and fear You. In Christ's name,

AMEN.

□ *Day 99:* 1 Kings 1–2
□ *Day 100:* 1 Kings 3–5
□ *Day 101:* 1 Kings 6–7
□ *Day 102:* 1 Kings 8–9
□ *Day 103:* 1 Kings 10–12
□ *Day 104:* 1 Kings 13–15
□ *Day 105:* 1 Kings 16–18

WEEK 16

1 KINGS 19–2 KINGS 13

Lord of the downcast in heart, we praise You for always being near to us! Though Elijah experienced a great victory over the prophets of Baal, the difficulties of ministering to individuals who never listened impacted him greatly. God, our hearts have been in a similar place as Elijah's. We look out and see a world filled with destruction and devastation. It often seems like we're alone. And yet, You continue to work. You have kept for Yourself individuals from all over the world who have not bowed down to the false gods and ideologies of this day. As we sulk, You continue to save sinners! Lord, remind us of this amazing truth. Comfort us in the power of the gospel. Encourage us to look up and stand up in faith. We ask this in Jesus' name,

AMEN.

1 & 2 Chronicles

"Haven't we been here before?" We've all thought this at one time or another. A place or situation just seems so familiar that it can't be our first time experiencing it, can it? Well, the books of 1 and 2 Chronicles can seem that way. After all, they cover a lot of the same history as the books of 1 and 2 Kings. They help us see a different perspective, and this is why they're important. Kings was written when God's people were in exile, but Chronicles was written after the remnant had returned to the land. Instead of explaining why God sent His people into exile, Chronicles tells us that God is not done with them. The Lord had not abandoned His people, despite their sin. They still had a future.

So the Holy Spirit inspired the author of

Chronicles to record the history of David's line, especially the kings who acknowledged the Lord and followed His law. It starts with eight chapters of genealogies. You and I might not immediately see much value in these genealogies. But for the ancient Israelites, these lists were important — especially this one. It starts with Adam and records the faithfulness of God to His people from the beginning. Surely this God will not abandon His people now.

After the record of the Lord's faithfulness to His people through the kings, Chronicles closes with the decree of Cyrus, king of Persia, to rebuild the temple in Jerusalem and let some of the Jews return. Why does this happen? Because Yahweh is faithful even when His people are faithless. He will keep His promises, including His promise to David that one of his descendants would always sit on his throne.

That's exactly what we have in Jesus. He is the descendant of David, the truly obedient One, the King we need. In the Hebrew Bible, the book of Chronicles is positioned last. When the people read or listened to it, they found themselves waiting for a King, waiting for the story to have a happy ending with the promised Messiah. Well, we aren't waiting anymore! Christ is ruling now, and He will never stop.

It's an Old Testament fact: as goes the

king, so go the people. Wicked kings led the people into sin, while righteous kings led the people into obedience. Jesus Christ will only lead us into righteousness. He has sealed the fate for all who trust in Him. He has won for us eternal life and a home in God's presence forever.

WEEK 17

2 KINGS 14–1 CHRONICLES 4

Oh, God, what do we do when things go from bad to worse? The kings of Israel were not following Your will. They devoted themselves to idolatry and mistreating their neighbors. Every king was worse than the one that came before him. Israel had gone so far down the path of idolatry, that You kicked them out of the Promised Land. When we choose the way of sin, help us to fall on our knees in repentance. We know You hear the words of those who are contrite, as with King Hezekiah, a good king in Judah. When he was exposed to his folly and sin, he pleaded before You and asked for forgiveness. Lord, give us such humility. Teach us to run to You rather than from You, that we may find rest for our souls

AMEN.

WEEK 18

1 CHRONICLES 5–26

Father, enlighten us when Your Word does not feel relevant to us. When we read name after name, our eyes can glaze over and our minds can wander. But these names reveal Your grand story of redemption. In every name we see Your promise made to Abraham long ago that You would give him a great nation. This promise is coming true! These names are a testimony to Your faithfulness. And yet, this is not the end of the story. These genealogies also remind us that we are waiting for David's Son, the One who would reign forever and ever, who would bless the world through His life, death, and resurrection. Thank You, Father, for using even genealogies to remind us that all Scripture is about Jesus. In His name we pray,

AMEN.

WEEK 19

1 CHRONICLES 27–2 CHRONICLES 24

Praise be to You, God, from everlasting to everlasting! Along with King David, we declare Your surpassing greatness and Your awesome power. Every good and perfect gift has come from Your hand, the greatest gift being eternal life through Your Son, Jesus Christ. We were once foreigners and strangers, forbidden to come before You as the God who is holy, holy, holy. But You have brought us near. Though we were once enemies, You have now called us sons and daughters. This is because David's son, King Jesus, has established Your kingdom and conquered our rebellious hearts. We want to go our own way, but Your Holy Spirit works in our hearts and gives us eyes to see and ears to hear. You are a kind and generous God. We praise You, for You are good, and Your love endures forever. In Jesus' name,

AMEN.

Ezra

Life in exile ... what a far cry from the glory years under David and Solomon! The people of God had been disciplined for their sin and faithlessness to their Lord. But God Himself was faithful, even gracious to them. He had vowed to bring them back to the Promised Land before He sent them into exile. Now that time had come.

Meanwhile, a lot had happened in the world of the Ancient Near East. Babylon was gone. The great empire that had conquered Judah and taken the Jews into exile had themselves been conquered by the Medo-Persians. And one day Cyrus, the Persian king, said, "*The LORD, the God of heaven, has given me all the kingdoms of the earth and he has appointed me to build a temple for him at Jerusalem in Judah. Anyone of his people among you ... may go up to Jerusalem in Judah and build the temple of the LORD, the God of Israel, the God who is in Jerusalem"* (1:2–3).

That's what is recorded in the book of Ezra. Under the leadership of Zerubbabel, thousands of Jews returned to their home, including many Levites and priests. They rebuilt the temple, but there was opposition. When the Persians were under different leadership, the rebuilding project was stopped for a while. But the Lord's purpose could not be stopped, and in time the temple was completed and dedicated. The Passover was celebrated again in Jerusalem. Finally, things seemed at least a little bit like they used to be. But this rebuilt temple wasn't as grand as Solomon's original version. *"Many of the older priests and Levites and family heads, who had seen the former temple, wept aloud when they saw the foundation of this temple being laid"* (3:12).

Ezra the scribe led another group to Jerusalem and helped to set things in order based on God's Law. The people were still waiting for something. God had remained faithful, but the glory of Jerusalem was less than it used to be. Though thousands of people were coming back to the Promised Land, many more still remained in the lands of their exile. The returnees were beginning to obey God's Law, yet their obedience was imperfect. They needed something more. The Messiah had been promised, and they were still waiting. That's where Jesus comes in! He is the final Temple of the God who dwells among us. Christ is the One who sustains His pilgrim people in exile on this fallen planet. He's the One who obeyed God's Law perfectly, earning a far greater salvation for us than merely a return to an earthly Promised Land.

WEEK 20

2 CHRONICLES 25–EZRA 10

God, You are a just and holy God. This is why Israel and Judah were judged and removed from the Promised Land. Though the kings of Israel were to lead the people in right worship and right practice, the kings as a whole were devoted to themselves and to idolatry. As the king goes, the people follow. But You were merciful. You preserved a remnant even as they were exiled to Babylon, and You promised that they would return home. You also provided them godly leaders like Zerubbable and Ezra. Though they were godly men, they were still sinful. We know that King Jesus is better. He is the greatest King, and as He goes, so His people follow, by the power of the Spirit. Give us the strength to follow our King and Savior, Jesus Christ. In His name we pray,

AMEN.

Nehemiah

Fourteen years. If a baby boy was born on the day Ezra
led his group of exiles back to Jerusalem, he would be 14
years old now. Nearly a decade-and-a-half is a long time.
And things had been happening, though not necessarily
good things. That's when Nehemiah, cupbearer to
Persian King Artaxerxes, heard the distressing news:
"*Those who survived the exile and are back in the province
are in great trouble and disgrace. The wall of Jerusalem
is broken down, and its gates have been burned with fire*"
(1:3). The returned exiles were still living in the ruins
of the Babylonian conquest nearly a century earlier.
The locals looked down on the Jews. This couldn't be
allowed to continue, not for God's chosen people!

So Nehemiah, under the favor of God Himself,
got the king's permission to go and rebuild Jerusalem.

And it wasn't just a physical rebuild! Ezra the scribe had
set things in order in the lives of the previous generation.
Now their children were back to the same old paths; they
were intermarrying with the unbelieving people around
them, something that in the Old Testament always led to
worshiping other gods and goddesses. So the Lord sent
another rebuilder, Nehemiah.

Just like when the temple was rebuilt
decades earlier, the Jews faced opposition from the
surrounding people. These people didn't want a
strong, separated Jerusalem in their midst. Walls
meant strength and separation. As with the first
temple, God watched over His people, and they
were able to complete the walls around their city.
A spiritual rebuild was under way, too. The people
confessed their sins, began to take care of the poor
again, and pledged to follow God's Law. But they
were still waiting for something better, as they'd done
in the book of Ezra. They were citizens of the earthly
Jerusalem, complete with a wall and a temple.

You and I are citizens of the New Jerusalem,
the one that Jesus Christ Himself has built and
prepared for us. He is our wall of protection. He is
our temple where we meet with God. And one day
He will return to set right the things that have gone
wrong. All of them.

Esther

Does God still care? Is He still in charge? Most
believers probably have asked similar questions.
What about when hard times come, or it seems like
our Lord is distant? Is He really still there, or has He
abandoned us? The book of Esther helps us answer
these questions. Remember, at this time the people
of God were in exile. They had disobeyed God so
thoroughly that He evicted them from His Promised
Land and sent them to Babylon. Then Persia took
over, and that's where Esther begins. King Xerxes
needed a new Queen. He had gotten rid of the last
one, Vashti, when she disobeyed his drunken request.

So right from the beginning we see that the
king of the Medes and Persians isn't really the one in
charge here. This pagan kingdom is under the Lord's

rule, whether it's immediately obvious or not. And in Esther, it isn't obvious at first. After all, God's name isn't used even once in the book! But His fingerprints are everywhere.

He caused Vashti to be deposed and an orphaned Jewish girl named Esther to take her place. Esther had a cousin named Mordecai who raised her after the death of her parents. He was used by God to discover a plot against Xerxes' life and was rewarded for his service. This led to an even more intense jealousy and hatred from Haman, one of the king's chief officials. He despised Mordecai already, but now Haman plotted to have Mordecai killed along with all his people, the Jews "*who keep themselves separate*" (3:8).

God's plans couldn't be stopped by this official in the Persian court. God used Esther to protect His covenant people. As Mordecai said to her, "*Who knows but that you have come to your royal position for such a time as this?*" (4:14). God's name wasn't mentioned. Though it seemed as if His people were going to be slaughtered while He remained silent, God was at work behind the scenes carrying out His plan through an unsuspecting Jewish exile named Esther.

No one expected that. That's what He did

with Jesus, too. For 400 years after the completion of the Old Testament, the Lord was silent. No new revelation came to His people. No prophets arose proclaiming His message, until angels began to appear and announce the births of John the Baptist and the Messiah Himself. God was silent, but He was still at work.

We can be confident that He's still working today, saving a people for His Great Name. And one day our Savior will return. Do you believe, even when times are tough?

Job

"The patience of Job" is a familiar saying. When you read the book of Job, you realize that "patience" is an understatement. Tragedies, trials, tribulations ... Job had them all. This book is part of the "Wisdom Books." Proverbs sets the stage, and then Job comes along and says that there is more to it than this. Just because you live in the fear of the Lord like Job did doesn't mean life will always go well for you. The book of Job shows this by telling us about a series of contests. The first puts Satan against God (1:6–12; 2:1–6); in the second Satan is against Job (1:13–22; 2:7–10); the third presents Job against God (3:1–42:6).

Satan claimed that Job only worshiped God because of what God gave him, not because God is God. God then allowed Satan to afflict Job with terrible trials and tribulations. The question is whether Job will stop worshiping and fearing God when God's blessings run out. We can think of this longest section in the book as Job's lawsuit against God. If you want a short summary of his complaint against his Lord, read Job 23. He claims that God is silent and far from him even though he has not committed a sin deserving this treatment.

This is where the book of Job begins to have a conversation with the book of Proverbs. Proverbs sets up the expectation that doing good leads to good things, and that doing bad leads to bad things. This is not a hard and fast rule, however. Nor is it a promise. Job is claiming that he has acted wisely (which he has), yet the second half of Proverbs' expectation has not worked out. In fact, it has been the opposite: Job has done good and received bad in response.

Job's three friends enter the scene. They do well when they are quiet and mourn with Job, but as soon as they open their mouths, they get into trouble. They think they know exactly what is wrong: he is clearly being punished for his sin, or perhaps for one particular sin. But then in Job 38, God appears to Job and challenges Job's mental power (38:1–39:30) and his physical might (40:6–41:34). Once God speaks, the issue is closed, and the lawsuit fades away into the wind. Job cannot say much in response to God's speech. He recognizes his place before God even though he did not receive an answer. He once again realizes who God is, and that God is powerful and trustworthy even if life does not make sense.

Job builds on Proverbs by reminding us that the one who receives good things is not necessarily wise or righteous, and the one who struggles is not necessarily foolish or wicked. This fallen world is a confusing place, and we need wisdom from God to navigate it. Job is presented as a blameless and upright man who feared and obeyed God. He suffered terribly, but not because of a sin he committed. Through the power of God, he persevered and saw many blessings come from God after the end of his ordeal. Essentially, he was God's champion, and in Job's struggle against Satan, Job prevailed.

After the trial was over, God commanded Job to act as a mediator and priest for the sake of his three friends who had sinned. This points ahead to Christ, the ultimate Champion of God who was completely and perfectly blameless and obedient yet suffered as no one had, either before or since. Christ defeated Satan, and after His work and ordeal were over, He was greatly rewarded by the Father. Jesus intercedes for His sinful people as their Mediator and Priest. Do you believe in this suffering, victorious Champion?

WEEK 21

NEHEMIAH 1–JOB 4

Oh, Lord, we thank You that You are faithful to Your covenant! If Your promises depended on us, we would have no hope of salvation. We are prone to wander and stumble in our spiritual walk. But You remain faithful. You promise to forgive. Even when we have been faithless, You remain faithful. This is not because we are so great in and of ourselves, but because You have promised to bless the nations through Abraham's seed, Jesus Christ. In Christ, every promise You have made has its yes and amen. In Christ, every pain will be healed, including Job's agony and ours. To read of Job's suffering pains us. But it comforts us to know that Jesus cares about our pain, since He too suffered. We're comforted to know that Jesus promises to make all things new.

AMEN.

WEEK 22

JOB 5–34

Oh, God, to whom would we look for comfort but You? You have given us Your Spirit to fill us with peace that surpasses understanding. When times of suffering come, it can be difficult. Job's friends started off well. They sat with suffering Job in silence. But then they spoke, thinking they were helping. Their long-winded speeches only made things worse. Lord, at times well-meaning people have made things worse in our lives. Forgive them. At other times, we have made things worse trying to help others! Please forgive us. Give us wisdom and the right words to say so that we may encourage those in need. When suffering comes, may we look to You, Jesus, our Lord who was acquainted with suffering and overcame suffering for our salvation. Remind us that in You, we find our rest. In Jesus' name,

AMEN.

Psalms

We're emotional creatures. That's how God made us. We feel and love. We desire and mourn. God created us body and soul, with a wide range of feelings. One of the great things about the book of Psalms is that it does not ignore our emotions. God wants every part of us, and that includes our emotions. The human author we associate most with the book of Psalms is King David. But he was just one of the writers along with Asaph, Moses, the sons of Korah, and several anonymous writers. Written in a variety of situations, the Psalms are the songs and prayers of God's covenant people.

The Lord was the Great King of Israel. When the psalmist addressed the Great King, sometimes it was to praise Him for who He is and what He has done. These psalms indicate a grateful contentment from the writer towards God, and they are full of praise from beginning to end. The psalmist had a clear view of things from his vantage point when writing; life made sense to him. Usually the psalmist calls the Lord's people to praise Him for His creation, His redemption, or both. Or the psalmist tells us the way of wisdom that we should follow.

Other psalms thank God for His help and deliverance. In these writings, the psalmist had been disoriented — feeling confused or lost — but now sees things more clearly. Many of these psalms express thanksgiving and gratitude to God for His deliverance. The reader can hardly help praising God alongside the psalmist. Several psalms are declarations of trust and confidence in the Lord.

Then of course, there are the psalms that are songs of suffering. The psalmist feels confused at best and lost at worst, life does not make sense to him, and he is crying out to the Great King for deliverance. In these sorrowful songs of pain and anguish, all but one (Psalm 88) have a pivotal point in the middle. In that verse, the psalmist stops crying out to God and instead turns to praising God.

In all of these types of psalms, the king is important. Will God remain faithful to the king? Will

the Lord allow the ruler of Israel to be defeated?
What kind of king would Yahweh give His people
to deliver them? And like the rest of the Old
Testament, the psalms point ahead to the Ultimate
King: Jesus Christ. Think of how beautiful it is that
Jesus took on flesh and came to earth, and therefore
grew up singing the psalms. We can be assured that
the psalms we sing and pray were also the songs and
prayers of our Lord.

  The book of Psalms really is all about Jesus.
Perhaps the best way to see that is to ask these types
of questions when reading Psalms: Does Jesus
offer atonement for the sin of His people, giving us
confidence of God's forgiveness? Does He suffer in our
place, lamenting even though He deserved blessing?
Is Christ the One deserving of praise for His work of
redemption? Does Jesus show us the way of wisdom as
the wise Son who obeyed for us? Is He being praised as
the King Israel needed who brought the Kingdom of
God with Him? Is Jesus the One who was rewarded by
God after His time of lamentation, earning blessings
for Himself and His people?

WEEK 23

JOB 35–PSALM 33

Oh, Lord our Lord, how majestic is Your name in all the earth! As You said to Job, You are the God who laid the foundations of the earth. You called forth the creation of the heavens, the earth, and all creatures that dwell in it. The sun, the moon, and the stars obey Your every command. You sustain all of life. And yet this does not compare to Your care for us. Who are we that You are mindful of us? You care for us, providing for all our needs. You nourish us through Your Word. Good Shepherd, You protect us from ravenous wolves, You make us lie down beside green pastures, and You lead us to still waters. You are a kind God. When we acknowledge our sins, You forgive us. What a great God we serve!

AMEN.

WEEK 24

PSALM 34–72

Father, something that we learn as we read and meditate on the Psalms is how wide-ranging these songs of praise are. When we are at the mountain top, we have songs to praise You for Your kindness and provision. When we are in the valley, there are psalms that acknowledge our pain as we continue to trust in You. These psalms testify of Your faithfulness and goodness to Your people, so that when our souls are downcast, we can remember how You brought us out of the grave and gave us life. You have sustained us when we are weak, stood by us faithfully in every situation, and sent Your Son to be the spotless sacrifice for our sins. We put our hope in You, and we praise You, oh marvelous God! We praise You, in Jesus' name,

AMEN.

☐ *Day 162:* Psalm 34–37
☐ *Day 163:* Psalm 38–42
☐ *Day 164:* Psalm 43–49
☐ *Day 165:* Psalm 50–55
☐ *Day 166:* Psalm 56–61
☐ *Day 167:* Psalm 62–68
☐ *Day 168:* Psalm 69–72

WEEK 25

PSALM 73–111

God of Israel, You have proven to be faithful to Your people in all times and in all places. You preserved the people of Israel in the midst of slavery. You delivered them from their oppressive captors through the use of amazing signs and wonders. You brought Israel out of Egypt and led them to the wilderness for a time, but You provided for them every day. Lord, as we wander in the wilderness for a time, waiting to enter the Promised Land that Jesus is preparing for us, we ask You to guide us. Protect us from sin, the world, and the devil. As temptations come from within us and outside us, hold us in Your grip and give us the strength to fight against these attacks. We love You, God, because You have delivered us and have promised to bring us home.

AMEN.

Proverbs

Wisdom. We all want it. But do you know where to find it? Do you even know what it is? Well, Proverbs is the book for you! It's part of what we call "The Wisdom Books" in the Bible, along with Job and Ecclesiastes. Proverbs sets the stage for the other two.

God has given us His law. We read His Ten Commandments, and they're pretty clear, aren't they? Murder is sinful. Coveting is wrong. God's law is black-and-white. But this sinful planet is often gray, and there isn't a command for every single circumstance in life. This does not mean that something is missing in God's law. It just means that we are often unsure what obedience to God looks like in a particular situation. So we need wisdom to live in this world as the Lord's people. The theme of the book of Proverbs is *"the fear of the LORD,"* which is the discipline to obey God in gratitude as His child. Before you can live wisely, you must have the fear of the Lord.

At the beginning of the book of Proverbs, we see a father teaching a son about life and wisdom. He is telling his son the differences between Lady Wisdom and Lady Folly. Proverbs is meant to cause a response, and the response the father wants his son to have is to follow and love Lady Wisdom while rejecting the advances of Lady Folly. Wisdom must be acquired; none of us are born with it. We must work at it. It grows and forms a person, often in a way that is not spectacular in our eyes.

When we consider this book, we might think of the two-line proverbs in chapters 10-29. We should remember that although Proverbs gives us wise principles, they are *not* hard-and-fast rules. Wisdom helps us to know how to glorify God day in and day out. Wisdom enables us to obey God's law even in a confusing world that often is more gray than it is black and white. Reasoning through things in the midst of life's difficulties and puzzles is a way to live as a child of God. Different times and situations call for different responses, which we can see in passages like Proverbs 26:4–5. Should we or should we not

answer a fool according to his folly? It depends on
the circumstances. Proverbs wants us to think deeply
about these things.

Proverbs teaches us that if we do certain
things, then we will have certain outcomes. We must
live in this world according to the way the Creator has
designed. Basically, Proverbs establishes the general
principle that doing good leads to good things and
doing bad leads to bad things. This is how the world
works because God designed it that way. There is
more to the story than this, however, which is where
Job and Ecclesiastes come in.

Ultimately, only Christ perfectly obeyed
God's law and acted in complete wisdom at all times.
Through the gospel, God forgives even our foolish
and unwise decisions because of Christ's work for us.
We are in *"Christ Jesus, who has become for us wisdom
from God — that is, our righteousness, holiness and
redemption"* (1 Corinthians 1:30).

WEEK 26

PSALM 112–PROVERBS 7

Father, we give thanks to You, for You are good, and Your love endures forever. Every day that we read Your Word, we see Your amazing love on display. It demonstrates to us that it is better to take refuge in You than to trust in humans. You will never fail us! Your Word is so wonderful and powerful that the longest song in the Bible is a song meditating on Your Word and law. Father, through Your Spirit help us to love Your Word more and more every day. Holy Spirit, show us how these Scriptures point us to the Lord Jesus Christ, the fulfillment of it all. Help us see that in the Bibles we hold and in the words contained there, we find Jesus. We pray this in the name of Jesus who gives us life for eternity and wisdom for today,

AMEN.

☐ *Day 176:* Psalm 112–118
☐ *Day 177:* Psalm 119
☐ *Day 178:* Psalm 120–133
☐ *Day 179:* Psalm 134–140
☐ *Day 180:* Psalm 141–150
☐ *Day 181:* Proverbs 1–3
☐ *Day 182:* Proverbs 4–7

WEEK 27

PROVERBS 8–29

Oh, great and wise God, all wisdom comes from Your hand. Kings and philosophers across the ages have sought to uncover the mysteries of this world, but You know them all. You were there at the beginning when the foundations of the world were formed. You spoke through Your Son, and it came to pass. Your Spirit blessed this work of creation by hovering over it. Father, Son, and Spirit, You are infinitely wise! And what's more, You have revealed Your will to us so that we may know what wisdom is. To fear You, oh God, is to have wisdom. Not as a thief fears the sun, but as a child fears a loving father or mother. Help us to grow in this wisdom, and to see that there's freedom found in fearing You. This fear is rooted in love and in a firm belief that You will never let us go.

AMEN.

☐ *Day 183:* Proverbs 8–11
☐ *Day 184:* Proverbs 12–14
☐ *Day 185:* Proverbs 15–17
☐ *Day 186:* Proverbs 18–20
☐ *Day 187:* Proverbs 21–23
☐ *Day 188:* Proverbs 24–26
☐ *Day 189:* Proverbs 27–29

Ecclesiastes

Ecclesiastes continues the conversation begun in Proverbs and Job. There is a way that God has set up creation, and Proverbs tells us that it's wise to live according to this created order. Job comes along and says there's more; just because someone is suffering doesn't necessarily mean that they've sinned against the Lord in some specific way. And now there is Ecclesiastes, the book that examines the differences between what we expect to happen in life and what actually happens. Ecclesiastes has a word for this: "Meaningless!" Things are often unexpected and nonsensical, and we cannot always answer the question "why did this happen?"

Ecclesiastes helps us to remember that the life of God's people is not free of pain, worry, confusion, and doubt. We do many things in our day-to-day lives that are pointless in the end. Ecclesiastes reminds us that things come and go, and death comes for us all (1:1–11). Life on this fallen earth is hard. Those who know God as Redeemer can feel a great tension between what they know to be true of their Lord and what they experience in His world.

This life is complicated, but wisdom is worth finding. In fact, sometimes having wisdom may not gain us much in a world under the curse. Having said all of this, the answer is to fear God and live, realizing that the pursuits of this life are not what ultimately satisfy.

Nothing in creation can give us what we truly want and need. Ecclesiastes points out the reality and inevitability of death. The only solution for this is to seek our satisfaction outside of creation, in Christ, who died for us. Because of Him, our death will be a homecoming to the perfect satisfaction of heaven instead of a sentence of eternal pain and absurdity. When we recognize the aging process and our approaching death, we should prepare for it with this in mind. This is how we live wisely even in a world that so often seems meaningless.

Song of Songs

"Song of Songs" may seem like a strange title for a book of the Bible. What it means is "the best song." This book celebrates the romantic love between a husband and wife, reminding us of some passages in Proverbs. Song of Songs is a series of love poems, teaching us about the goodness of sex in the context of God's ordained institution of marriage. The language is descriptive yet dignified; there is no reason to feel shame about that which God has created and approved. To enjoy the gift of intimacy with one's husband or wife is to live wisely. A wise person will seek to have such a relationship with his or her spouse.

But this book is about more than just earthly romantic relationships. It also points to God's love for His people. Or to use New Testament language, it shows us more clearly Christ's love for His Church. Throughout the Bible God's people are described as His bride. The Lord of the universe has set His love upon us, and we are in a relationship with Him. A good marriage shows us a picture of Christ's love for us. And Christ's love for us shows us a picture of what our love for our spouse should be.

The Apostle Paul says in Ephesians, *"Husbands, love your wives, just as Christ loved the church and gave himself up for her to make her holy, cleansing her by the washing with water through the word, and to present her to himself as a radiant church, without stain or wrinkle or any other blemish, but holy and blameless. In this same way, husbands ought to love their wives as their own bodies. He who loves his wife loves himself"* (5:25–28). This is the love our Savior has for us. How could we not respond to Him in love?

Isaiah

Many people hear the word "prophet" and immediately think of a person who tells the future. The prophets in the Bible are more than this, however. It was through the prophets that God revealed His heart to His people. Some prophets, like Elijah and Elisha, did not write books. Others did write what God had revealed to them, the most well-known of which are Isaiah, Jeremiah, Ezekiel, and John (in the book of Revelation).

Prophets were called by God, and this meant something quite spectacular. God would send the prophets to His covenant people in His place as His messengers. Basically, they were His covenant lawyers He used to sue His people. Do you recall what Israel said when God made a covenant with them at Mt. Sinai? *"Everything the LORD has said we will do"* (Exodus 24:3). But they failed, again and again. The Lord had told them what would happen if they kept disobeying: they'd be exiled out of the Promised Land, evicted. The prophets reminded them of the consequences if they did not repent.

Isaiah did exactly that. God called him to be His mouthpiece to His people. It was a long, often thankless calling. The ruthless Assyrians were the big dog on the block back then. Soon they'd destroy the northern kingdom of Israel, and Judah wouldn't last much longer. Even though Isaiah repeatedly told the people about God's judgment if they didn't repent, most of them didn't listen. Eventually, the threat of exile became a certainty. They had gone too far.

But Isaiah wasn't just a prophet of doom. The Lord also gave him words of comfort and grace, words that told His people about the gospel and the coming Messiah. God was going to send servants. Some, like the Persian King Cyrus, would lead His people back from exile. But the Ultimate Servant would be the Messiah, Jesus. The One who is *"holy, holy, holy"* (6:3) would Himself come and save His unholy people.

Only because of Jesus can we have confidence to come into the presence of the Holy One of Israel.

He is the Servant who was completely obedient yet experienced God's judgment in our place. Because of Him, we will never be exiled from God's presence. He's our Immanuel, God with us ... forever.

WEEK 28

PROVERBS 30–ISAIAH 3

Our Lord of Wisdom, thank You for showing us the way, even as we wrestle with the complexities of life. You've shown us that wisdom is found not in our relationships, not in our pursuit of status and things, but in our devotion to You and Your Word. Help us to fear You, Lord, and to obey You, even when it is difficult. In our relationships, help us to honor You and keep Your all-sufficient love as our foundation. Thank You for showing us that in Christ You've paved the way for us to know Jesus and wisdom. Fill us up with that wisdom, we pray, and send us out to proclaim Your good news to the world. All for Christ's sake, and for His glory,

AMEN.

WEEK 29

ISAIAH 4-31

Our great and almighty God, You have always known that Christ would come to rescue us from sin and darkness. You sent prophets to call Your people to faith, and to show them the way. Jesus is the Messiah, the One who was promised to provide a feast of well-aged wine. Thank You for sending Christ who turned water to wine in Cana. Our Savior keeps His promises. Thank You for not leaving us alone and for sending Jesus to provide everything we need. In Him we will find hope and salvation, and in Him alone we will feast together in the last days. We have no need to fear Your judgment or Your anger. All we have to look forward to is Your love and grace in the light of Christ for the rest of our days. Thank You! Help us to grow and to trust. Help us to believe Your promises. All in Jesus Christ's marvelous name,

AMEN.

WEEK 30

ISAIAH 32–52

Oh, Lord, we need Your comfort. You told Your prophet Isaiah to comfort Your people, and we need Your comfort even now. Life is difficult; it always has been. And in our sin we realize how desperate we are for Your grace and mercy. Comfort us with the love of Christ, the Messiah that You promised so many years ago. Help us to rest in His love, to receive peace in Him. Help us trust in Your Christ-fulfilled promises. They are yes and amen in Him. Help us to find comfort and strength in the One who suffered and died in our place. Turn us from our attempts to save ourselves so we can receive Your grace to comfort us in our trials and tribulations. You are the God who cares. Help us rejoice in Your love.

AMEN.

Jeremiah

After Isaiah's death, things went from bad to worse in the kingdom of Judah. The end hadn't come yet, but it was on its way. That's when the Lord appeared to a young priest named Jeremiah and told him, "*Before I formed you in the womb I knew you, before you were born I set you apart; I appointed you as a prophet to the nations*" (1:5). And what a situation Jeremiah was walking into! The people of Judah were still rebelling against God. Much like us, they found it was easy to trust in things other than their Lord. They were drawn almost magnetically to foreign powers, the outward motions of religion, even the false gods and goddesses of their neighbors.

Despite the fact that these sins were leading to judgment, God still spoke words of promise and grace to His people. In fact, that's one thing that really stands out in this book: Yahweh will remain faithful to His promises even when His chosen people are faithless. The Lord said through Jeremiah, "'*The time is coming,' declares the LORD, 'when I will make a new covenant with the house of Israel and with the house of Judah ... I will put my law in their minds and write it on their hearts. I will be their God, and they will be my people. No longer will a man teach his neighbor, ... saying, Know the LORD, because they will all know me, from the least of them to the greatest,' declares the LORD. 'For I will forgive their wickedness and will remember their sins no more'*" (31:31, 33–34). There was hope, even though the exile was coming.

In the meantime, however, the people kept rebelling against the God of their fathers. They truly deserved what was coming to them. And Jeremiah himself would live to see his prophecies of doom come to pass. The Lord's judgment was not far off. Would God make a new covenant with His people? Was it even possible for Him to forgive their wickedness and remember their sins no more? Yes, because of what Jesus came and did in the place of those who trust in Him. We're no better than the ancient Jewish people. We have committed many of the same sins. As the Lord said, *"My people have committed two sins: They have forsaken me, the spring of living water, and have dug their own cisterns, broken cisterns that cannot hold water"* (2:13). But Jesus is faithful even when we are faithless. He bore the wrath that we deserved when He faced the ultimate exile — death on a cross for the sins of His people. And if you trust in Him, you have no reason to doubt your relationship with God. He has forgiven your wickedness and will remember your sin no more.

WEEK 31

ISAIAH 53–JEREMIAH 8

Before the world was even created, You knew our name, oh, Lord. You called us out of darkness and set us on the path of righteousness that we might glorify Your name with our lives. Help us to remember Jesus, our suffering servant, the Messiah who came. Though His people didn't see anything in Him to praise or worship, He came to save them. He came to save us! Help us to trust in Him and to find salvation in His name alone. Help us, like the prophets, to accept Your calling on our lives. Use us to glorify Your name and to draw many people to Your Son.

AMEN.

WEEK 32

JEREMIAH 9–30

Oh, Lord, Your wrath and judgment are fearful things. Yet Your judgment never comes upon Your people without hope. Exile meant suffering, but You didn't send Your people into exile without a promise of return and redemption. With You, suffering and death never get the final word. Help us remember this when times are hard. Help us continue to trust in Your promises. We need Jesus more than we know. In our sin we attempt to save ourselves more times than we care to admit. Help us, Lord. Redeem us. Give us a safe return to the beautiful abundance of Your grace. All these things are ours not from our own power, but because of Jesus. Help us to remember that weakness is strength in Your kingdom. Mold us to love and trust. In Christ's name,

AMEN.

WEEK 33

JEREMIAH 31–49

Gracious and heavenly Father, thank You for giving us a new covenant — not like the one that was given to our ancestors in the faith, but new and grounded in Jesus Christ. Thank You for welcoming us into Your household, to belong to Your people, to be called sons and daughters of the Most High. Your grace fuels our entire life. And it's Your grace that shields us from judgment. Too often we try to earn our way into Your covenant by following rules. Forgive us. We forget that You've already welcomed us through the blood of Jesus. Help us to trust and follow Him with the new hearts You've given. Help us to remain steadfast, not because of our own strength, but as we rest in the strength of Christ our Redeemer.

AMEN.

Lamentations

Exile had come. After decades of hearing about it, God's judgment finally fell on the southern kingdom of Judah. Babylon had come with her army, surrounded Jerusalem, and penetrated her walls. God's people saw death and destruction in a whole new way. There were survivors, one of them the prophet Jeremiah. He was in an unenviable position: writing the book of Lamentations after his prophecies of judgment came to pass. The wrath he had proclaimed was here. His mournful tone already in 1:1 is evident: *"How deserted lies the city, once so full of people! How like a widow is she, who once was great among the nations! She who was queen among the provinces has now become a slave."*

Truthfully, Judah deserved this. Repeatedly they
had sinned against God, disregarding the Lord's
prophets and even killing some of them. Jeremiah
himself ministered in the kingdom for years
without success. But if all of this was true, then
why didn't Yahweh destroy them down to the last
man? Because He is merciful and faithful.

Even in the midst of the death and
destruction in Jerusalem, Jeremiah saw the
Lord's goodness. He said in chapter 3, *"Because
of the LORD'S great love we are not consumed,
for his compassions never fail. They are new every
morning; great is your faithfulness. I say to myself,
'The LORD is my portion; therefore I will wait
for him.' The LORD is good to those whose hope is
in him, to the one who seeks him; it is good to wait
quietly for the salvation of the LORD"* (v. 22-26)

Wait for the salvation of the Lord — that's
what Jeremiah and the faithful remnant of Judah
had to do. It would be hundreds of years before
Jesus, the answer to Jeremiah's prayer, would
arrive on the scene. He took the full wrath of
God that we deserve for our sins. Through faith
in Him, we are saved from ever experiencing the
Lord's judgment. Even if life is hard and tragedy
comes to us, we have a Savior in heaven. He's

coming back to make all things new and wipe
every tear from our eyes. Great is His faithfulness!

Ezekiel

Lamentations tells us about when Judah and
Jerusalem were destroyed by the Babylonian empire
in 586 B.C. But this wasn't the only time Jewish
people had been forced from the Promised Land.
In fact, the exile happened in stages, with the final
conquest of Jerusalem being just the last part of
God's judgment on His rebellious people. The
prophet Ezekiel was a priest who was part of one of
the earlier waves of exiles on their way to Babylon.

In the Book of Ezekiel, we read of strange
visions and rituals. But the overall point is clear:
God is withdrawing His presence and His blessings
from His people. Ezekiel has a vision of God's
special presence leaving the temple and the city of
Jerusalem. *"The glory of the LORD went up from*

within the city and stopped above the mountain east of it" (11:23). Judah was slowly dying as God's blessings dried up. God was bringing judgment on Judah and Jerusalem (chapters 1–24).

Still that wasn't the end of the story. The Lord also would punish the nations around Judah, those who had been her enemies and had taken advantage of her suffering (chapters 25–32). Ultimately, judgment would not have the last word. Yahweh will bring blessings to His people. The exile won't be the end of the story (chapters 33–48). The Lord's people need His presence to live, and that's what they'll get.

In Ezekiel 37, we read the famous vision of the Valley of Dry Bones. Ezekiel said, *"This is what the Sovereign LORD says to these bones: 'I will make breath enter you, and you will come to life. I will attach tendons to you and make flesh come upon you and cover you with skin; I will put breath in you, and you will come to life. Then you will know that I am the LORD'"* (v. 5–6).

God is in the business of creating life in the midst of death. And that's exactly what He did 2,000 years ago on a cross outside of Jerusalem. God the Son, the Lord of all Life, died for the sins of His rebellious people. Because of that, all who

trust in Him will have life — everlasting life. The
dry bones will live forever with their Savior.

WEEK 34

JEREMIAH 50–EZEKIEL 12

Oh, Lord, You are worthy of praise because You've called us out of the world and have given us a new identity. As we look around us, we can't help but see Your good creation with its men, women, and children all made in Your image. Yet we see brokenness — in the world and in our own hearts. We know we need redemption. The brokenness that we see and feel is meant to lead us to You. Help us return to You, Lord. Help us love and live as You've called us. Then the nations will know that You are the Lord, for You've told us in Your Word that Your glory comes through Your acts in the world. What greater act than the love of Christ poured out for us, and the victory of Christ over the grave! Help us be people of the Messiah.

AMEN.

WEEK 35

EZEKIEL 13-30

Time and time again, Lord, You sent prophets to Your people not only to warn them, but to call them to a better way. Forgive us for neglecting their message. The grand visions of judgment and wrath overwhelm us. But help us not to turn away, because in these visions we also get a glimpse of what our Savior went through on the cross. He took on our sin and bore the judgment we deserve. Our sins are wiped clean because of His love, not because of us. We are sinners; He is not. Your judgment for sin reminds us of its severity. It reminds us that we cannot save ourselves. Only the Messiah can save, the One who gathers us from all over, and who proclaims Your promises. Help us believe them. Then we will know that You are the Lord.

AMEN.

WEEK 36

EZEKIEL 31–48

We need new hearts, Lord. We know we do. Our sin reminds us every day that we fall far short of Your glory. Our hearts of stone don't respond to Your Word. They don't reach out in love to our neighbors. In our sin we are just like the valley of dry bones: dead, unloving, uncaring. Yet, Your Spirit can make us live! Please help us receive the life offered to us in Your gospel, the message that brings dry bones to life and moves them in love and loyalty to the Lord. Turn our stone hearts into flesh, Lord, and write Your Word on our hearts. We need Your grace to mold us and move us. Flood us with Your Spirit. Empower us to proclaim Your good news to those around us. Make us one, a people united under the banner of Jesus.

AMEN.

☐ *Day 246:* Ezekiel 31–32
☐ *Day 247:* Ezekiel 33–35
☐ *Day 248:* Ezekiel 36–38
☐ *Day 249:* Ezekiel 39–40
☐ *Day 250:* Ezekiel 41–43
☐ *Day 251:* Ezekiel 44–46
☐ *Day 252:* Ezekiel 47–48

Daniel

We all know stories from Daniel. He interpreted dreams; he survived the lions' den. But do we know much about the book named after him? These stories are only a part of a bigger story, after all!

Daniel was one of the people taken away from Judah *before* the final destruction of both Jerusalem and the temple. In fact, he went into exile even earlier than Ezekiel. Daniel was a hostage taken by the Babylonians, kept in Babylon in order to keep Judah in line. It's more difficult to rebel if some of your countrymen and family members are living in the enemy's capital city. Or at least, that was the thought. It didn't work, of course. Judah rebelled and was eventually destroyed. But while Daniel the hostage was in Babylon, the Lord began to move in some unexpected ways.

Daniel was one of many Jewish young men trained for service to the Babylonian king, Nebuchadnezzar. In the book of Daniel, the pagan kings are important. Why? Because even though the big empires of the day were having their way on the international scene, Yahweh was still in control. Even when His people went into exile, they did so at God's own command. Sometimes this comes through when the human king commanded one of God's children to do something against His Law. The Lord showed His power when He saved the three exiles in the fiery furnace or when He kept Daniel alive among the ravenous lions. That's what we see again and again in the first half of the book: God is in control of history as it happens.

He is the Great King above all other kings. He watches over His beloved children. King Nebuchadnezzar himself came to realize this after God made him live like a wild animal for a time. But even when Nebuchadnezzar left the scene and the Babylonians were replaced by the Persians, Yahweh remained on His throne.

In chapter 7 the book takes a turn: Daniel is one of the Lord's prophets, and he receives prophecy after prophecy and vision after vision. The Lord shows His prophet the future, and in the future He will remain in charge. Ultimately, He will bring in *"one like a son of man"* who will receive all authority and power over the nations of the earth (see 7:13–14). This was fulfilled by Jesus, and one day *"at the name of Jesus every knee should bow, in heaven and on earth and under the earth, and every tongue confess that Jesus Christ is Lord, to the glory of God the Father"* (Philippians 2:10–11). This is our Savior. We can be confident that He is watching over us as He rules all the kingdoms of the earth.

Hosea

It was a marriage like no other. But that wasn't a good thing! The prophet Hosea was Yahweh's last messenger to His faithless people, the northern kingdom of Israel. God gave this prophet some unusual instructions. We read in chapter 1:2, "*Go, take to yourself an adulterous wife and children of unfaithfulness, because the land is guilty of the vilest adultery in departing from the LORD.*" Being married to an adulterous spouse was what the Lord Himself had experienced. Back in Exodus, He made a covenant with Israel, that He would be their God and they would be His people. But as He was still giving the Law to Moses, the people were at the base of Mount Sinai worshiping a golden calf. Idolatry on the wedding night!

For the rest of Israel's history, there were ups
and downs. But by this point there were only downs.
Israel had mostly forsaken her Lord for generations.
Her kings led her in sin. Her false temple was a
stumbling block. And the prophets of the Lord
weren't getting through, not even Hosea with his
bizarre object lesson. The names of the children
from this marriage strike us as strange: Jezreel, Lo-
Ruhamah, and Lo-Ammi. Through those names,
God told Israel He would soon punish them. Hosea
couldn't be sure that these children were actually
his, and in a similar way the people of the northern
kingdom were no longer God's people. They had led
the marriage right off a cliff and were about to be
destroyed, exiled, and scattered by the Assyrians.

But there's good news in Hosea, as surprising
as that sounds. Though the people were unfaithful,
the other party in the marriage is the Faithful One,
Yahweh Himself. It's helpful to remember that God
chose a man named Hosea as His prophet, since
that name basically means "*Yahweh has saved.*" And
Yahweh would save! The northern tribes of Israel
would never come back from exile.

But God was not done with His people. He
promised He would save them, and that's exactly
what He has done through Jesus Christ. Jesus

bought us back from our slavery to sin just like Hosea bought his wife back from her bondage. Our Savior gathered those who were scattered into every tribe, tongue, and people and brought them into God's very presence. He loved us enough to die for us, and we are His people. Forever. This relationship *cannot* be broken.

WEEK 37

DANIEL 1–HOSEA 14

Oh, Lord, we are so prone to wander. Yet You continually come to us. You won't let us go. No matter how insistent we are on leaving, You steadfastly pursue us to the end. Thank You for saving us from ourselves and for loving us despite our sin. Just like Daniel and his friends, we live in a world that doesn't understand or like Your people. Our world can be hostile. Yet You call us to faithfulness. Help us remain true to Your Word, even in the difficulties we face. We need Your strength. We know You hear us, and we know You promise to strengthen us always. In Christ's name,

AMEN.

Joel

Some of us like insects and bugs more than others.
But we've all been annoyed with them. The ancient
people of God had a different relationship with
these creatures, especially the locusts. Since farming
was such an important part of their life, a drought
or fire could mean hard times until the next season.
A swarm of locusts would do the same — eating and
devouring until there was nothing left.

The people of God were experiencing
hardship. They continued to disobey their Lord, and
He was bringing an army to discipline them. But
unlike the armies He brought during the times of the
Judges, this army wasn't human. An army of locusts
would bring God's judgment on His rebellious
people. The prophet Joel tells them that this swarm

is just a preview of the Day of the Lord when Yahweh will bring judgment to the entire planet.

As we've come to expect by this point, God always gives hope. "*I will repay you for the years the locusts have eaten ... You will have plenty to eat, until you are full, and you will praise the name of the LORD your God, who has worked wonders for you*" (2:25–26). That's our comfort and hope, too.

God says He will "*pour out my Spirit on all people*" at the end of days. The only way to experience this is to be in a proper relationship with Him, a relationship of faith. The Apostle Peter quoted from Joel 2 when he preached his famous Pentecost sermon urging his listeners to put their faith in Jesus.

Jesus is the answer to the problem of the book of Joel. He has brought the Day of the Lord to us, at least as a preview. We have the Holy Spirit poured out on us, giving us confidence that the Lord will protect us on the final day of judgment. We need not fear when our Judge is also our Savior.

Amos

Things are not always what they seem. Sometimes the brand new car is a lemon that needs constant repair. Or the friendship that once seemed so vibrant and strong goes sour. That's sort of what happened to ancient Israel. The northern kingdom was experiencing a time of prosperity with things going pretty well ... or so it seemed on the surface. Unfortunately, there was rot and mold underneath.

Amos was a prophet of the Lord to the northern kingdom. He seemed to be a typical hardworking, blue-collar guy. Flattery and fake politeness weren't his style. And that's exactly how God used him. First, he began to prophesy against the nations around Israel. You can imagine how his fellow countrymen felt about that! Then the bad news hit closer to home. When he began to prophecy against Judah for her sins, things got downright uncomfortable. But through Amos the Lord turned His words toward Israel. They had been just as disobedient as these other nations which would soon experience God's judgment and wrath. What's worse, Israel and Judah had the Lord's own Law. They had sinned against more than their neighbors when they turned their back on God and began mistreating their fellow Israelites. Death and destruction were coming, and in Israel's case they would be here in three short decades. Life was about to get a whole lot worse.

Though God's people were more satisfied with the blessings Yahweh gave them than they were with Yahweh Himself, their covenant God was not done with them. *"I will restore David's fallen tent ... so that they may possess the remnant of Edom and all the nations that bear my name"* (9:11–12). God's judgment started outside of Israel and Judah and worked its way in.

In Jesus Christ, the blessings and salvation of the Lord have gone in the opposite direction. It's not unlike Jesus saying to His apostles, *"You will receive power when the Holy Spirit comes on you; and you will be my witnesses in Jerusalem, and in all Judea and Samaria, and to the ends of the earth"* (Acts 1:8). That's why you and I can experience the grace of God today. The gospel of Jesus has gone out to the ends of the earth. Even to us.

Obadiah

Well, this was different. Obadiah was a prophet of
the Lord, but not one who prophesied to Israel or
Judah. Instead, Obadiah was God's messenger to the
people of Edom. We know next to nothing about
Obadiah. And the book that shares his name is only
one short chapter.

But we *do* know about Edom. They were the
offspring of Jacob's brother, Esau. When Babylon
came and attacked Judah, devastated the land, and
took many Jews captive, the people of Edom turned
on their relatives and plundered the ruins. Judah was
already down and out when the Edomites poured
salt on the wound. But they bit off more than they
could chew. Attacking God's people, even in the
midst of their judgment, was like trying to attack God

Himself. And the Lord does not forget. Edom would soon come to an end, never to rise again, while Judah returned from exile a generation later. Edom took the Lord's wrath while Judah experienced His salvation.

It will be the same on the Last Day. "*The day of the LORD is near for all nations. As you have done, it will be done to you; your deeds will return upon your own head*" (v. 15). The only way of escape is to rely on the grace and mercy of Jesus Christ. When He returns, "*on Mount Zion will be deliverance*" (v. 17). Jesus is the One who brings blessings to us, the sinful people who deserve judgment. Because of our Savior, we are transformed from Edom to Judah. And salvation is ours!

Jonah

Sometimes things seem out of place. A palm tree in the snow. Ice cream in the produce aisle. An ancient Hebrew on the Mediterranean Sea. That's what we find in the book of Jonah — an Israelite prophet running to the sea instead of doing what God had commanded. Jonah's story is a familiar one to us, and also one that speaks directly to us today.

The Lord came to His prophet Jonah and told him to bring a message against Nineveh, the capital city of the Assyrian Empire. But Jonah fled. Why? Because he knew that Yahweh is gracious, and if the Assyrians repented, they wouldn't be punished. After all, the Assyrians were known for their brutality. Armies often did terrible things in those days, and Assyria stood out from the rest. Jonah wanted

Nineveh to get what they deserved. So he decided to not bring God's message to them. Instead, he boarded a boat headed for Tarshish, the exact opposite direction from where the Lord had sent him.

The sea meant chaos for ancient Israelites. It was seen as a sure way to die. It seemed like that's what would happen to Jonah: he'd be killed in the great deep for disobeying the Lord. But God brought a great fish to swallow Jonah, and after Jonah prayed, the fish spit him up onto dry land. The animal was more obedient than the prophet!

Finally, Jonah went to Nineveh to preach God's Word. And wouldn't you know it, they repented and believed! This angered Jonah. The bizarre ending to the book is meant to show us that the Lord is more willing to bring His salvation to the ends of the earth than we often are. He is a compassionate God. We see that clearly in the life, death, and resurrection of Jesus Christ for all who believe in Him, Jew or gentile. Repent and trust in Christ, and you will be saved as surely as the ancient Ninevites!

Micah

These were strange times. Both the northern kingdom of Israel and the southern kingdom of Judah were having ups and downs. Assyria grew stronger on the international scene, making all non-Assyrians nervous. Though Israel had turned their back on Yahweh more thoroughly than Judah had, God was coming to bring judgment to the entire kingdom.

That's what Micah came and proclaimed to the people during the same time that Isaiah was prophesying in Judah. They had reached the point of no return. Even if they repented now, it would be too late. The capital of the northern kingdom was Samaria, and the Lord promised to *"make Samaria a heap of rubble"* (1:6). Assyria was coming, no matter what the false prophets told the people. And would the southern kingdom have a happier ending? No, not at all. The prophet Micah foretold, *"Jerusalem will become a heap of rubble"* (3:12). Both capital cities were heading for destruction.

As is common in the prophets' words, there is also salvation mixed in with the judgment. In chapter 4 we read, *"They will beat their swords into plowshares and their spears into pruning hooks. Nation will not take up sword against nation, nor will they train for war anymore"* (v. 3). War was coming to Samaria and Jerusalem, but war would not have the last word.

Why? Because of what the Lord promised to a small town in Judah: *"But you, Bethlehem Ephrathah, though you are small among the clans of Judah, out of you will come for me one who will be ruler over Israel, whose origins are from of old, from ancient times"* (5:2).

Hundreds of years later Jesus Christ was born in Bethlehem. He is the King we need, the Shield who stands between us and judgment because He took our condemnation on Himself. And He leads His people in righteousness and justice. He enables us to act justly, love mercy, and walk humbly with our God (see v. 6:8). That's why His kingdom is different than Israel or Judah. A perfect kingdom can only be ruled by a perfect King. We are citizens of that kingdom only through faith in that perfect King. Do you believe?

WEEK 38

JOEL 1–MICAH 7

Heavenly Father, You promised in Your Word that the time of Christ would be marked by men, women, and children prophesying in Your name. You said You would pour out Your Spirit on all flesh and draw many to Your Messiah. Thank You that we live in that time even now. Men, women, and children proclaim Your gospel daily as they profess faith in Jesus Christ. We need Your Spirit every moment these days to strengthen us in our devotion. Help us become men and women that are marked by Your grace, who live out our faith every day. Help us be like dew from the Lord among the nations, refreshing all those around us. Help us be Your light in this dark world, that many might come to know Your saving grace. In Christ's name,

AMEN.

Nahum

Like Obadiah, Nahum's prophecy was directed to someone other than Israel and Judah. The Lord sent Nahum to proclaim His anger against Nineveh. Why Nineveh? Well, it seems the repentance that happened under the ministry of Jonah didn't last very long. Although even the animals were put in sackcloth in those days, soon enough it was brutal business as usual in Assyria. And Yahweh was coming in judgment.

This is what He says through Nahum: "*The mountains quake before him and the hills melt away. The earth trembles at his presence, the world and all who live in it. Who can withstand his indignation? Who can endure his fierce anger? His wrath is poured out like fire; the rocks are shattered before him*"

(1:5–6). For all their power and might, Assyria would soon be wiped off the face of the Ancient Near Eastern world, never to rise again.

Nahum's name means "comfort." But how can this message be comforting? Because God's people could know that this judgment was coming to those who had so horribly mistreated them. Their Lord is King over all the earth and will not let the guilty go unpunished. As King, not only will He punish the guilty, but He also will rescue the downtrodden, those who can't save themselves. "*The LORD is good, a refuge in times of trouble. He cares for those who trust in him*" (1:7).

Jesus Christ is the One to whom we flee for salvation. He is a refuge for all who trust in Him. Why? Because He took the wrath that His people deserved. He suffered in a way that Nineveh could scarcely understand. And one day He's coming back. It will be a time of judgment for His enemies but complete salvation for all who call on His name. They'll never be persecuted again. Are you trusting Him?

Habakkuk

"Picking you up and making you feel good!" It seems like every town has at least one radio station with that tag line. We want to feel good, upbeat, and happy as if we didn't have a care in the world. But that isn't how it always goes. The book of Habakkuk doesn't immediately strike you as one that picks you up and makes you feel good. Yet the words of this prophecy are comforting to God's people.

We don't know much about Habakkuk. As with many of the other minor prophets, he suddenly appears to speak the Lord's words and then disappears almost as quickly. But we know some of his words quite well, especially those about faith.

Habakkuk was sent by Yahweh to the people of Judah when they were committing great evil against each other and against their Lord. Listen to Habakkuk's harsh complaints to the Lord: "*Why do you make me look at injustice? Why do you tolerate wrongdoing? Destruction and violence are before me; there is strife, and conflict abounds. Therefore the law is paralyzed, and justice never prevails. The wicked hem in the righteous, so that justice is perverted*" (1:3–4). In Habakkuk's despair, he feels that God seems less concerned for justice than he the prophet does.

Everywhere Habakkuk looked, he saw wickedness, from God's people and from the Assyrians alike. But the Lord saw it too. The Babylonians were His tool to destroy the Assyrians once and for all. And they were coming for Judah next. The injustices would not be allowed to stand. Sadly, that just made Habakkuk more upset. Yahweh was going to punish Judah using a nation even more wicked than Judah. Was there no hope whatsoever? Would there be no justice? God's answer is clear: Babylon wouldn't escape judgment, either. The Lord had not changed. He was still righteous and would act justly.

On a hill outside of Jerusalem 2,000 years ago, God the Son hung on a cross for sins He didn't commit. Yet this was God's judicious and sovereign solution to the problem of sin. Christ paid our penalty. He was crucified by the great power of the day, the Romans. Because of that, one day *"the earth will be filled with the knowledge of the glory of the LORD as the waters cover the sea"* (2:14).

In the meantime God's people are to trust in Him and in Christ's work in our place. As the Apostle Paul says in Romans 1:17, quoting Habakkuk 2:4, *"The righteous will live by faith."*

Zephaniah

Surely things would start looking up, right? Josiah
was king in Judah. The Book of the Law had been
rediscovered. Would that mean crisis averted? No,
not really. The people didn't change everything.
And the reforms would prove to be short-lived.
So Yahweh sent another prophet, Zephaniah (a
descendent of King Hezekiah), to announce the
Lord's coming judgment.

Judah, Philistia, Moab, Ammon, Cush,
Assyria ... none of them would be able to stand when
Yahweh came in His battle armor. The judgment He
was about to pour out on these nations was just a
preview of the Day of the Lord, the Day of Judgment.
And what will that day be like? *"In the fire of his
jealousy the whole earth will be consumed, for he will*

make a sudden end of all who live in the earth" (1:18). No one would survive this. Maybe the closest thing we can think of today is a nuclear explosion. There's no making it out alive if you're there when the bomb goes off. And this bomb is going to go off over the entire planet.

So is there any hope? Yes, because the Mighty Warrior will turn His sword against those who trouble His people. He will eliminate the haughty boasters and save the meek and humble. When that happens, He "*will purify the lips of the peoples, that all of them may call on the name of the LORD and serve him shoulder to shoulder. From beyond the rivers of Cush my worshipers, my scattered people, will bring me offerings*" (3:9–10).

You and I are evidence that God has been in the business of saving an international people for His Great Name. Jesus came, died, rose again for His people, and then sent His apostles to proclaim this message to the ends of the earth. The church has been doing that for nearly 2,000 years now. The same earth that will see God's judgement come to every nook and cranny will also see Christians coming to the Lord from every tribe and nation. Because of Jesus, we can be confident to "*trust in the name of the LORD*" (3:12).

Haggai

Most of the prophets God sent to His people prophesied before the exile, warning about the Lord's imminent judgment. Some came to His people while they were in exile in Babylon. Haggai arrived a bit later. He was sent to the people of Judah who had returned to Jerusalem. Despite this return, not everything was going as it should have.

    The Lord asked His people this question through Haggai: "*Is it a time for you yourselves to be living in your paneled houses, while this house remains a ruin*" (1:4)? They still needed to rebuild the temple, but also needed a kickstart after all this time of opposition and distraction. Judah's governor, Zerubbabel, was a descendent of King David and an ancestor of Jesus, David's Greater Son.

Yahweh was remaining faithful to His old promises.

So in chapter 1 God commands His people to rebuild His house, and in chapters 2 and 3 He gives them encouragement. Some of the most beautiful words from the Old Testament prophets are found in this book. *"This is what the LORD Almighty says: 'In a little while I will once more shake the heavens and the earth, the sea and the dry land. I will shake all nations, and the desired of all nations will come, and I will fill this house with glory,' says the LORD Almighty... The glory of this present house will be greater than the glory of the former house,' says the Lord Almighty. 'And in this place I will grant peace,' declares the LORD Almighty"* (2:6–9).

Centuries later Jesus Christ would come, the Ultimate Temple where God dwells with man. This God-Man would come to this same temple in Jerusalem so that the glory of the second, lesser temple would be even greater than Solomon's original version. God the Son Himself came here! He made the temple obsolete, however, because He is the once-for-all sacrifice for our sins. Now He intercedes for us as our High Priest. Rather than making sacrifices in a temple, we now worship the God who came and dwelt among us. In fact,

He's building us into a temple! As the Apostle
Paul says, "*In him the whole building is joined
together and rises to become a holy temple in the
Lord. And in him you too are being built together to
become a dwelling in which God lives by his Spirit*"
(Ephesians 2:21–22).

Zechariah

When we read about visions in the Bible, they're often filled with fantastic imagery. The visions of Zechariah are no exception. Satan accusing the high priest in God's throne room, a flying scroll, a woman in a basket ... the book of Zechariah contains some strange passages!

So what exactly was the Lord telling His people through this prophet? To understand that, we have to know *when* and *where* Zechariah was sent. This man came as Yahweh's mouthpiece to the people of Judah who had returned to the land. He ministered during the same time as Haggai, and he dealt with some of the same problems — issues with rebuilding the temple.

The visions that Zechariah saw were meant

to both comfort and challenge the returned exiles. This was accomplished by showing the importance of the temple itself. Rebuilding the temple was a daunting task, but it would be worth it because this is where Yahweh promised to dwell with His people in a special way. The people needed to repent of their faithlessness and to remember what God's presence meant: blessing and the fulfillment of His promises to His people. The Lord returned to Jerusalem as He promised in 1:16: *"I will return to Jerusalem with mercy, and there my house will be rebuilt."* One day this city would be the center of a worldwide pilgrimage. *"The survivors from all the nations that have attacked Jerusalem will go up year after year to worship the King, the LORD Almighty."*

In a way, this is what's happening right now. People from every nation, tribe, and language are coming to salvation in the name of Jesus Christ. He is Immanuel, God With Us. The first two temples were always pointing to Him in the first place. In Jesus Christ, God had come to dwell with us, and He'll never leave.

What does that mean for us as we wait for the Day of the Lord of which the prophets foretold? It means we are like the priest Joshua told of in chapter 3: *"Now Joshua was dressed in filthy clothes as he stood before the angel. The angel said to those who were standing before him, 'Take off his filthy clothes.' Then he said to Joshua, 'See, I have taken away your sin, and I will put rich garments on you.' Then I said, 'Put a clean turban on his head.' So they put a clean turban on his head and clothed him, while the angel of the LORD stood by"* (vv. 3–5).

The people in Zechariah's day needed to know that God forgave their sins so that they could have confidence while they rebuilt the temple. We need to know that we are covered in Christ's perfect, spotless righteousness as we wait for His return, where He will dwell in our presence forever. Even now, we can have confidence that the Holy Spirit is dwelling within us because of Christ's work for His people. God's special presence is here.

WEEK 39

NAHUM 1–ZECHARIAH 14

Oh, Lord, You are slow to anger but great in power. We need to take this to heart. In Your wrath You could wipe out the entire planet in a moment, yet You withhold. You are great in power, yet You use Your power to turn hearts toward You. Thank You for saving us so mightily! No one can stand before You, yet You make Yourself known to us and bring us near. You truly are good, Lord. You are a stronghold in the day of trouble, and we have had so many. You've promised to protect us. In Christ, You have given us access to Your shelter. In our suffering and despair, You are with us and protect us. Help us praise You in all things and rest in Your unfailing grace. In Christ's name,

AMEN.

Malachi

We all know that a famous coach's farewell press conference or a political leader's last speech in office are moments for the history books. We might even look back fondly on these words. But God's last words ... well, that's completely different! The book of Malachi gives us a remarkable closing to the Old Testament.

God's people — at least some of them — had returned from exile. Ezra and Nehemiah were history. The prophets Haggai and Zechariah were nearly a century in the past. The temple and walls of Jerusalem were still standing. But now what? Yahweh had promised to do wondrous things *with* and *for* and *in* His people when He promised to bring them back generations before. But they were still waiting for those blessings. The Jews were starting to wonder, doubt, and go astray. They had broken their covenant with God. Again! That's what led to the exile in the first place!

So what will the Great King do? "'*I will send my messenger, who will prepare the way before me. Then suddenly the Lord you are seeking will come to his temple; the messenger of the covenant, whom you desire, will come,' says the LORD Almighty*" (3:1). This will be a time of purifying, and the Lord will spare the faithful remnant of His people.

Sure enough, hundreds of years later angels began showing up and announcing first the birth of John the Baptist, and then the birth of the Messiah Himself. Jesus came to His temple where the purification started and will continue until the Day of the Lord. Malachi told the people in his day to trust in Yahweh and remain faithful to Him. He calls us to do the same in our day. Trust in Christ. Remain faithful to Him. He will finish what He started 2,000 years ago. Malachi is the last book of the Old Testament, but it isn't the end of the story. It's just another chapter in the great story that's all about Jesus.

NEW TESTAMENT

Matthew

400 years of silence. That is what the people of God experienced between the end of the Old Testament and the coming of Christ. During this time, the Persians were conquered by the Greeks who were in turn replaced by the Romans. Things were moving and shaking in the world. Still, no new word from God came to His people. That is, until the Lord Himself announced the arrival of the Messiah. The Gospel of Matthew begins with a genealogy as does the book of Chronicles, the last book in the Hebrew Bible. Basically, Matthew is telling his readers that this is the next chapter in the same story. It's the great story, and it's all about Jesus!

The whole Old Testament pointed ahead to Christ's birth, life, death, resurrection, ascension,

and Pentecost. It will culminate in the Second
Coming. God the Son came to earth and took on
flesh in order to save a people for His name. As
Immanuel, *God With Us*, Jesus Christ is true God
and true man, and He will remain true God and true
man forever. All four gospels tell the story of His
birth, life, death, and resurrection. But each looks
at it from a slightly different angle, similar to Kings
and Chronicles telling the same story with different
goals in mind. See if you aren't struck by something
different as you read through each gospel book.

The Gospel of Matthew, written initially for
first-century Jewish readers, would show Jesus as the
continuation of the Old Testament story and the
fulfillment of God's law. In fact, Matthew quotes
the Old Testament more often than any other New
Testament author. This gospel is structured around
five sermons by Jesus, just as the Old Testament
began with the five books of Moses.

Jesus is the Prophet, Priest, and King we
have always needed. As the Ultimate Law Keeper,
Jesus obeys where Adam and Israel disobeyed. As
the sacrifice for sins, He redeems His people from
something much worse than slavery in Egypt:
condemnation and death.

Moses, the Passover lamb, the Torah, King

David, the kingdom of Israel — all of these were signposts pointing ahead to Jesus. And now He's here! That's the message that Matthew gives to us. Christ is our Savior and Teacher. There's no one else like Him. The Kingdom of Heaven has come.

WEEK 40

MALACHI 1–MATTHEW 17

Heavenly Father, Your people sat waiting and hoping for hundreds of years. Thank You that You keep Your promises. You are always faithful; You always have been and always will be. You've shown us again and again that You never let Your people down. Jesus teaches us that we are blessed, loved, welcomed, and called into Your family and Your kingdom. We see Your all-encompassing compassion as He heals and feeds Your people. Help us be people that follow in His path. Help us be true disciples that take up our cross, pray in secret, and do not let our left hand know what our right hand is doing. Help us to glorify You as we seek Your kingdom first, and trust You to add the rest. In Christ's name,

AMEN.

☐ *Day 274:* Malachi 1–4
☐ *Day 275:* Matthew 1–4
☐ *Day 276:* Matthew 5–6
☐ *Day 277:* Matthew 7–9
☐ *Day 278:* Matthew 10–11
☐ *Day 279:* Matthew 12–13
☐ *Day 280:* Matthew 14–17

Mark

As terrible as war can be, sometimes it's necessary. There are places in Scripture where the Lord presents Himself as a warrior who fights for His people and against His enemies. The Gospel of Mark paints a similar picture. It has much in common with Matthew and Luke. But there are differences, too. For one thing, Mark was writing as a traveling companion of the Apostle Peter, so we can assume his gospel has Peter's fingerprints on it in some ways. Much of the dialogue in Mark is probably from Peter's own memories of what Jesus said and did during His earthly ministry.

Mark was writing to Christians in Rome who were beginning to suffer for the faith. He tells them about the suffering Savior, the Son of Man who invaded the wilderness, Galilee, and Jerusalem with the good news of the gospel. Mark told how Christ's suffering leads to ultimate victory for Himself and for all those who trust in Him. But just because the victory has been won doesn't mean the people of God won't suffer.

Still, we can be confident in our afflictions. Jesus suffered and then was victoriously glorified. The same will happen to us because of Christ's work. We know our pain will end, and we will one day be glorified with our Savior. The Son of Man has made us children of God. The invasion was successful. The war is won, even if it isn't over yet.

WEEK 41

MATTHEW 18–MARK 5

Oh, Lord, we confess that too often we are preoccupied with constantly comparing ourselves to those around us. We need to hear Your words yet again to come to You as a little child. Like children, we are needy. Like children, we are vulnerable. Like children, we are dependent upon another to provide and care for us all the days of our lives. Help us remember our frailty and our need for grace. Help us remember that You came down to make Yourself vulnerable and weak. You died so we might live. Help us trust in Your gospel. Send us to into the world to make disciples and spread the light of Your Word. Thank You for loving us, and thank You for giving Jesus for us. In Christ's name,

AMEN.

Luke

You'll see variety in the kinds of writing in the New Testament. There are histories, prophecies, poems, letters. But one thing is pretty standard: the human authors of the books were Jewish. All of them except Luke the physician, that is. And this gentile basically wrote a two-part gospel: the first part, which we know as *The Gospel of Luke*, tells us about the birth, life, death, and resurrection of Christ; the second part, which we know as *Acts* or *The Acts of the Apostles*, tells us about how the ascended Christ continued to minister on the earth through His Holy Spirit and apostles.

So what is the theme of the Gospel according to Luke? The gentile physician sets up the story of Jesus as a great journey. Most of the beginning of the book records Jesus' journey in Galilee, where He taught parables about the Kingdom of God and performed miracles. But Galilee was never meant to be the final destination. What was the point of God the Son coming to earth? Jesus tells us clearly when He spoke to the tax collector, Zacchaeus, "*The Son of Man came to seek and to save the lost.*" In fact, at different times in Luke we read a particular word in reference to why Jesus came. In the Parable of the Prodigal Son it's translated as "*had to.*" Luke used this word to identify Christ's mission on earth. He *had to* come and save sinners.

That was always the goal. And that meant Jesus was never going to just stay in Galilee. His journey had to continue. Our Lord traveled to Jerusalem, teaching and performing miracles along the way, showing His power over diseases and demons. Certainly, He would wield His power over sin, too, when the time came. Jesus was welcomed into Jerusalem in triumph, but less than a week later He hung on a cross outside the city. He did not remain dead; the journey continued.

One of our favorite passages of Scripture at *Haven Today* comes from a journey: a walk to Emmaus. In Chapter 24 we read that the resurrected Jesus disguised Himself and met two of His followers. These two believers were discouraged and downhearted due to the events of the weekend—the Messiah had been killed! But we read that Jesus kept teaching them: "*Beginning with Moses and all the Prophets, he explained to them what was said in all the Scriptures concerning himself*" (24:27).

The journey didn't end on the cross. And it didn't end in Jerusalem. Jesus ascended to heaven. His gospel has gone to the ends of the earth, and He's coming back to take us with Him for one last, great journey.

WEEK 42

MARK 6–LUKE 2

Your gospels teach us, Oh Lord, that Christ's love knows no bounds. There never was and never will be anyone too far from the reach of Your grace. Through Jesus' feeding the crowds, healing individuals, and casting out demons, You show us how deep Your love for us is. Thank You for Your Word which shows the love of our Savior pouring forth time and time again. When Jesus came to His disciples out in the middle of the sea, they learned then and there that You are a God who treads upon the waves and calms any storm. Help us remember Your goodness and greatness in the midst of our struggles. Remind us that Your grace provides all we need. Ultimately, help us remember Your death and resurrection. Like the women at the end of Mark, help us be brave to proclaim Your good news.

AMEN.

☐ *Day 288:* Mark 6–7
☐ *Day 289:* Mark 8–9
☐ *Day 290:* Mark 10–11
☐ *Day 291:* Mark 12–13
☐ *Day 292:* Mark 14
☐ *Day 293:* Mark 15–16
☐ *Day 294:* Luke 1–2

WEEK 43

LUKE 3–18

Heavenly Father, too often we are like the prodigal son in Luke 15, demanding Your blessing only to run off and waste it on our own selfishness and sin. We turn away from You to live our lives in extravagance and indulgence, only to reach the end of ourselves in pain and misery. Or we act like the older son, consumed with our own obedience and earning our place. We forget the most important commandments, to love You with our entire being and to love our neighbor as ourselves. Help us remember Your love which welcomes the wayward child and accepts us unconditionally. Move in our hearts to choose the way of Jesus and trust in Him and His work for us, not in ourselves. For Your sake and Your glory — not ours — and in Christ's name,

AMEN.

☐ *Day 295:* Luke 3–4
☐ *Day 296:* Luke 5–6
☐ *Day 297:* Luke 7–8
☐ *Day 298:* Luke 9–10
☐ *Day 299:* Luke 11–12
☐ *Day 300:* Luke 13–15
☐ *Day 301:* Luke 16–18

John

Do you remember playing matching games as a kid? The point was to find cards that were identical to each other. And of course, one of the easiest ways to figure out which two cards are identical is to find the ones that are different. Once you eliminate those, you're well on your way!

The four gospels in the New Testament aren't exactly identical. But they share similarities. Or to put it another way — they aren't copies of each other, but they sure do rhyme! Matthew, Mark, and Luke are similar, including many of the same events and sayings. But the Gospel of John is the odd one out. It's still similar to the others but rarely would be confused with them.

The Apostle John — brother of James and

one of the sons of Zebedee—wrote this book with a very specific goal in mind. He said, *"Jesus did many other miraculous signs in the presence of his disciples, which are not recorded in this book. But these are written that you may believe that Jesus is the Christ, the Son of God, and that by believing you may have life in his name"* (20:30–31). John wants us to know that Jesus is the only Savior.

So how does John begin this gospel book? By telling us the theme: Jesus is the Word of God, and Jesus is God. The rest of the book proves this. John spends the first 12 chapters proving that Jesus is God, not just a carpenter from Nazareth, but the Son of God come in the flesh. He tells us how Jesus saves us by His death and resurrection. John also reminds us that Jesus promised to send the Holy Spirit to His followers. So as you read, ask yourself this question: Do I believe that Jesus is the Messiah, the Son of God, and that by believing, I have life in His name?

WEEK 44

LUKE 19–JOHN 8

Oh, Lord, in the Bible You tell us that You are the Word and that Jesus is the divine Word, the One who was not only with You at the beginning but also who is divine Himself. He's the Word who became flesh and dwelt among us. This is the Jesus we serve and follow, who turns water into wine and feeds thousands as the true bread of life. Thank You for sending Jesus to save us, forgive us, and accept us into Your heavenly kingdom. Thank You that in Christ we have a home, and a place to call our own. Help us reflect Your glory in our own lives. Help us know the love that You have for us and share it with those who are in pain or have yet to hear of Your grace. In Christ's name,

AMEN.

Acts

Imagine you are assembling a piece of furniture. You were making progress, and it was looking more like it should. But then the instructions became complicated, and you lost your place. You scratch your head, wondering, now what?

We might feel that same way at the end of the four gospel books. We've read about Christ's birth, life, death, resurrection, and ascension into heaven. But now what? Where do we go from here? How did we get from the disciples staring up at the ascending Jesus to the gospel and the church being found in every corner of the world? The book of Acts answers those questions.

The book of Acts (which could be called the Gospel According to Luke, Part 2) begins with

the heavenly ascension of Jesus and ends with the
Apostle Paul in a Roman prison. That's a period
of roughly three decades, ten times as long as the
earthly ministry of Jesus which comprises most
of the gospel books. During these 30 years, Luke
records how the gospel of Jesus Christ has gone
to the ends of the earth. After all, the theme of
the book is that Jesus is still at work through His
Holy Spirit and through the apostles. As small
and powerless as the church may seem humanly
speaking, there is divine power behind it.

Before Jesus ascended to the Father's
right hand in heaven, He gave instructions to His
apostles. These instructions are the outline of Acts.
Christ said, *"You will receive power when the Holy
Spirit comes on you; and you will be my witnesses in
Jerusalem, and in all Judea and Samaria, and to the
ends of the earth"* (1:8). In Acts 1-7, the apostles,
led especially by Peter, spread the gospel in the city
of Jerusalem. When persecution began, the young
church was scattered throughout Samaria and Judea,
with the church of Christ expanding with it.

In chapter 9, everything changes. One of
the foremost persecutors of the church, a Pharisee
named Saul, is converted by Jesus Himself on the
road to Damascus. Referred to as Paul in the rest

of the New Testament, this new Christian was
sent by Jesus as His apostle to the gentiles. As an
instrument of the Lord, Paul brings the gospel to the
ends of the earth. He goes on missionary journeys,
planting churches in places where Jesus had not
been proclaimed. He mentors young pastors and
helps churches deal with problems. He suffers and is
eventually killed for his faith.

Wherever you may be reading this right now,
the gospel has probably come to your corner of the
earth because of what God did through this Jesus-
hater-turned-Jesus-proclaimer. This is the grace of
God! This is what the gospel of Jesus does!

WEEK 45

JOHN 9–ACTS 3

Lord, when Your Holy Spirit fell upon Your disciples, You unleashed a power in Your people that changed the world forever. Your gospel has gone forth to the nations, and we are so grateful that it has reached us. Thank You for giving us access by Your Spirit to the throne room of grace and sending us into the world with Your message. Jesus is the way, the truth, and the life. Help us follow His path, believe His Word, and experience His life as we trust in You day by day. This life is difficult. Jesus knew it would be, so He gave us peace that we can experience daily as we live into the calling You have on our life. Thank You for saving us. Help us be the kind of people You desire. In Jesus' matchless name,

AMEN.

WEEK 46

ACTS 4-17

Heavenly Father, we believe in Jesus today because Your disciples were faithful to proclaim it far and wide. Even in the face of persecution, Your gospel went forth and changed hearts throughout the world. You saved even one of the worst enemies of the truth, the Apostle Paul, who sought to murder Christians and destroy Your Church. Lord, Your power is boundless, yet You use it to change hearts and to bring many into Your kingdom. Thank You that You have brought us in; thank You for Jesus and for the life we have in His name. There is no other name under heaven that You have given by which we may be saved. Help us to be the kind of people who are ready to proclaim Your good news to those around us. Help us be a light for Christ wherever we go. In Jesus' matchless name,

AMEN.

Romans

One of the most frequently studied and well known books in the entire Bible is Romans. And for good reason! The epistle of Romans is where we see Paul explain the gospel of Jesus in more detail than anywhere else in the New Testament. But what is an "epistle," anyway? Contrary to popular opinion in first-grade Sunday school classrooms everywhere, the epistles are not the wives of the apostles! An epistle is basically a letter, which is what most of the books in the New Testament are. Paul alone wrote 13 of them. The letters of the New Testament are written to churches or individuals to explain and interpret what happened in the Gospels and Acts. They also apply what Jesus has done to our lives.

In the book of Romans, Paul is writing to

a church he has never visited (although he knows many of these Christians already). Since he has never preached to this congregation before, he wants to tell them what his message is. And that's what he does for 16 chapters!

Paul begins with his theme for the book: "*I am not ashamed of the gospel, because it is the power of God for the salvation of everyone who believes: first for the Jew, then for the Gentile*" (1:16). But before he gets to the good news of Jesus Christ—the gospel itself—he has to remind his readers about the bad news of sin and judgment. He looks at different groups of people, from those who have never heard the gospel to Jews who have the entire Old Testament. His conclusion for all people outside of Jesus Christ is that "*all have sinned and fall short of the glory of God*" (3:23).

This is where the gospel comes in as the power of God that brings salvation to sinners, whether Jew or gentile. He brings us from death to life, from condemnation to acceptance, all through Jesus. Before Paul concludes the imperatives of his letter, he breaks into praise to God: "*Oh, the depth of the riches of the wisdom and knowledge of God! How unsearchable his judgments, and his paths beyond tracing out! 'Who has known the mind of the Lord?*

Or who has been his counselor?' 'Who has ever given to
God, that God should repay him?' For from him and
through him and to him are all things. To him be the
glory forever! Amen" (11:33-36).

    So how should this change how we
live? Well, that's the third section of Romans:
the imperatives. Those who have experienced
this amazing grace from God should act like it.
Christians should live like Christians. We have been
forgiven and loved, so we should forgive and love
others. That's the Christian life in a nutshell. It
begins and ends with Jesus. Are you as confident in
the gospel of Christ as the Apostle Paul was?

WEEK 47

ACTS 18–ROMANS 7

Oh, Father, as we walk through Your glorious gospel, we are reminded of our own frailty. You created us good. You created us to know You and to love those around us. Yet we find ourselves failing. You created us to be a beacon of hope in a dark world, but we repeatedly slink back into the darkness of our own sin. We see the effects of sin everywhere. Our weakness and Your goodness are meant to bring us to repentance, but we often slide into despair. Heal our sick hearts, Lord. Help us to come to repentance, trust in Your kindness, and love our neighbor. You've freed us from the power of sin; help us to live like it. By Your Spirit, help us live lives that show we now belong to Jesus Christ. In His name,

AMEN.

1 Corinthians

"A mess" is an accurate description of the church
in Corinth. The Greek city of Corinth itself had
a lot going for it, at least by outward appearances.
It was known as one of the most impressive
cultural centers of the day. It would be like living
in New York or Los Angeles today — lots of things
happening and always something to see. But from
a spiritual perspective, things were not going well.
The prosperity of the area led to many of the same
problems we see today: greed and selfishness.
Corinth was full of pagan temples where idols were
worshiped daily, and sexual immorality was an
integral part of it all.

Of course, these issues were spilling over
into the church. When we read Paul's epistles to

the Corinthians, it's as if we're hearing one side of a phone call. We know what Paul is saying, but we don't always know the specific details that led him to say it. Still, we can learn a lot from this book. The Corinthian Christians were spiritually immature. They had gotten themselves into one mess after another with lawsuits, sexual immorality, careless talk, and misunderstandings about the resurrection. But the Lord was still faithful to them.

Through the Apostle Paul, God gave corrections and instructions to this church. One of the main themes of the letter is still important for us today: love your brothers and sisters; give yourself to them even if it means challenging them and calling out their sin. Though this is the opposite of what the world considers "love," it's exactly the type of love that Christians are called to have for each other.

Jesus, our great example, loves His own, even when we're unlovely. He doesn't just wink at our sin—in fact, He came to earth to deal with it once and for all. In Chapter 15 Paul gives us a beautiful summary of the gospel: "*Christ died for our sins according to the Scriptures, that he was buried, that he was raised on the third day according to the Scriptures, and that he appeared to Peter, and then to the Twelve*" (vv. 3-5). Because of this good news, we who trust in Jesus have our sins forgiven and have received the Holy Spirit. Therefore, we're able to obey our God, sincerely if imperfectly, as we are being remade into the image of the Savior.

WEEK 48

ROMANS 8–1 CORINTHIANS 16

Heavenly Father, we've seen in Your Word some of the greatest passages ever written for the human race. We've read that nothing, not life or death, not sin or Satan, can separate us from Your unfailing, all-powerful love in Christ Jesus. Your love teaches us to be humble and sincere, to be sensitive to our neighbor, and to make every effort to make peace with them. Your love saves us from our inabilities and our stubbornness. It frees us to be the kind of people You call us to be in Christ, marked by a desire to glorify You and to see Your grace in Jesus. Help us to love others even as You have loved and radically transformed us. In Jesus' name,

AMEN.

2 Corinthians

The Corinthian believers had received Paul's first
letter, and they had even begun to correct some of
the concerns he wrote to them about. But everything
wasn't solved. Not yet. There were still problems
in Corinth. For one thing, they had swung the
pendulum too far when it came to church discipline.
In 1 Corinthians, Paul rebuked them for not acting
when one of their members began an inappropriate
relationship with his own stepmother. Apparently,
they had acted now, but when this brother repented,
they wouldn't welcome him back! Isn't that just like
us? First we think grace means sin is acceptable, then
we're corrected and begin to doubt if God's grace
can really reach any sinner.

But even beyond this problem with

discipline and accepting a repentant sinner, there was something deeper going on. The Corinthian church was having an authority crisis. Some people in the church claimed they were teachers, even going so far as to declare themselves apostles. But they were leading believers astray. Paul had harsh words for these deceivers: "*Such men are false apostles, deceitful, masquerading as apostles of Christ. And no wonder, for Satan himself masquerades as an angel of light. It is not surprising, then, if his servants also masquerade as servants of righteousness*" (11:13–15). Because of this, Paul spends a lot of his time defending his ministry, specifically defending that he was directly called by Jesus as one of His apostles.

Since Paul had been called by the resurrected Christ Himself, his message can be trusted. It's a message about giving. Our Savior gave Himself for us, and so we ought to be generous with one another. Paul gave a lot. He tells the Corinthians about the suffering he had experienced as a messenger of the gospel — nearly dying many times, being imprisoned, flogged, beaten, shipwrecked, stoned, sleep-deprived, cold, hungry, and desperate. Chapter 11 spares very little detail about Paul's constant danger and sufferings. On top of it all was the daily pressure of his concern for all the churches.

But Paul knew that Christ and His gospel are worth it, so he was willing to give up his earthly comforts to make Jesus known. Are we?

Galatians

Paul begins his letter to the Galatians in a peculiar way. *"I am astonished that you are so quickly deserting the one who called you by the grace of Christ and are turning to a different gospel"* (1:6). Typically, Paul began more softly, even if there were real problems in the church to which he was writing. But the situation in Galatia was different: they were beginning to believe something other than the gospel of Christ.

Do you remember Paul's theme in his epistle to the Romans? He was not ashamed of the gospel, because it's the power of God for salvation. He had preached this same gospel to the Galatian Christians. In fact, he may have even planted these churches! But what happened at some point after Paul left?

They abandoned the gospel, and Paul wasn't having it. As he says in 4:11, "*I fear for you, that somehow I have wasted my efforts on you.*"

So what exactly was the problem? We don't have a full picture of the false teaching that had infected the Galatian churches. But it seems a group of people we call "Judaizers" were deviously, slyly undermining the work of Jesus. The Judaizers probably could not have fooled the Galatians if they came to them and said, "Hey, we have something better than Jesus!" But false teachers are rarely that straightforward. Instead, they told the Galatians that they needed Jesus, plus a little extra. Specifically, they needed to keep the ceremonial laws, like circumcision, from the Old Testament. That's what would give them the last push to cross the spiritual finish line. In other words, these agitators were telling the Galatian people that they needed to believe in Jesus *and* keep the law for salvation.

Confidently, Paul reminds them of the same thing he once preached to them in person: when it comes to Jesus as Savior, He's either a complete Savior or no Savior at all. If we could somehow save ourselves by keeping the law, then why did Christ have to come? And if everything we need is found in Christ, then why add anything to Him? "*If righteousness could be gained through the law, Christ died for nothing"* (2:21)!

Jesus is the Savior of sinners. Jesus alone. Don't look to anything else, even things that might be good. We are called to do good works, after all! We should love God and our neighbors. But our love and obedience do not save us, not even a little. Our salvation begins and ends with Jesus. Have you begun to abandon the gospel? Jesus Christ is the only Savior. There's no other Name under heaven by which we may be saved.

Ephesians

We all know the church exists, and we understand that it's important. But why, is it so important? How did we get from God the Son — who took on flesh, lived, died, rose, and ascended — to a group of people from every tribe, tongue, and nation? Was this part of God's plan all along? If you've ever asked questions like this, then Ephesians is the book for you. Ephesians is one of Paul's prison epistles (along with Philippians, Colossians, and Philemon), written while he was under arrest by the Roman authorities. Similar to his epistle to the Colossians, Paul references his house imprisonment only briefly here and there.

So how does he begin this letter? Think of it as time-traveling to the time before time. Paul reminds his hearers that God has loved His people since *"before the creation of the world"* (1:4). That's why Jesus came to redeem those who believe. This was the plan all along. Man with his sinfulness has never been in charge here. God was not caught flat-footed. Salvation was always meant to come to us. This ought to confirm for us that God doesn't love us because Jesus died for us. No, Jesus died for us because God loves us.

It's His love that brings all of these blessings to us, whether we are Jew or gentile. Christ's death brought the two together into one people of God. Most of the Ephesian believers were probably gentiles, just like most modern believers are gentiles. But we can be confident that both receive the same Christ by faith. It's the same salvation. We're part of the same church. That's the only true, lasting peace we can expect in this world.

Since God has done such wonderful things for us in Christ by the power of the Holy Spirit, it should change how we live. The power we need to defeat sin in our lives comes from the Holy Spirit — the same God who has all power. Our confidence and hope is that Christ lived and died for us. So we ought to live and, if necessary, die for Him in gratitude. How could we not? He's the One who made us alive when we were dead. He's the One who died for us, His enemies. He's given us what we need to live the Christian life. Think about the famous armor of God in Chapter 6. What does it include? Truth, righteousness, readiness, faith, salvation, and the Word used by the Spirit. All of these are blessings of salvation which the Lord has given to us. Let's use them.

WEEK 49

2 CORINTHIANS 1–EPHESIANS 6

Oh, Lord, You draw near in all our sufferings and all our troubles. You come to our aid, You lift us up, and You comfort us through Your Spirit. Our sickness, our pain, and our own sin racking us with guilt can seem like too much to bear. Yet You draw near. You comfort us, though not for our sake alone. You comfort us so we might be able to comfort others. How wonderful it is that we can receive Your grace and be used by You to comfort others! You have chosen us as Your workmanship and given us access to Your throne room, all because of Jesus. Thank You for sending Jesus to save us with marvelous resurrection power. Help us to live into that power and love those around us, not for our own glory but for Christ's. In Jesus' name,

AMEN.

Philippians

Philippians, the Epistle of Joy, was written by a prisoner. Though it sounds contradictory, that's what we have in this short but powerful book. Basically, the imprisoned Paul tells the Philippian believers that God is still able to give them joy in the face of persecution and struggle. Paul himself is evidence of this!

He begins in Chapter 1 by telling the Philippians that as long as his imprisonment advances the gospel of God, he will be filled with joy. After all, Jesus suffered and humbled Himself, even to the point of dying on a cross. And because of His life, death, and resurrection in our place, we are enabled to imitate our Savior's humility and love with joy, even while going through trials.

Paul explains in chapter 3 the reason for his confidence and joy: "*I consider everything a loss compared to the surpassing greatness of knowing Christ Jesus my Lord, for whose sake I have lost all things. I consider them rubbish, that I may gain Christ and be found in him, not having a righteousness of my own that comes from the law, but that which is through faith in Christ — the righteousness that comes from God and is by faith*" (vv. 8-9).

No one and nothing could take away his joy because no one and nothing could take away Christ. Since we have the same Christ, we can say along with Paul, "*I have learned to be content whatever the circumstances*" (4:11). Trials and struggles will come, but you have Jesus, and He will never leave you nor forsake you. So rejoice and live a life worthy of the gospel!

Colossians

Paul had never visited the church in Colossae, but he was still concerned for their spiritual well-being. And they had a problem. A religious movement sometimes referred to as the "Colossian Heresy" was tempting the Colossians. We don't know all the details of this false teaching, but we know what Paul said in response to it.

It seems it was some sort of Jewish mystery religion mixed with Christianity. Basically, cults like this would take parts of Judaism, Christianity, and the pagan religions of the day and throw them all together. These false teachers were commanding and forbidding what God had not commanded or forbid. They were tempting Christians to look elsewhere than to Jesus alone for salvation. But

Christ has already earned all the blessings these false teachers promised, and more!

Because this was an attack from inside the church rather than from outside, it was much more devious. That's why Paul was so concerned. He wrote this epistle while he was in prison, probably around the same time he wrote Ephesians (these two letters are very similar). He wanted to impress upon the Colossians the supremacy of Christ and the sufficiency of His gospel. He encouraged them to press on in understanding this sufficient good news. It was bearing fruit and increasing throughout the entire world. The Old Testament prophecies concerning the gentiles were coming to pass before their very eyes, just as they are today.

But if these things are true, then how do believers become filled with the knowledge of God's will in all spiritual wisdom and understanding? The answer is simple: through reading and hearing God's Word. This is where He has revealed His will to us. We must be content with it, and we must continually go back to this source of knowledge, wisdom, and understanding. Paul wanted the Colossian Christians to live out who they already were: people who were forgiven and redeemed through Jesus Christ. What we need isn't to move on to something better, but to have a better understanding of the supremacy and sufficiency of Christ and His gospel. We need to realize who Jesus is and what He has done for us. The gospel is enough because Jesus is enough. He is supreme over creation and redemption. This is our hope.

How can we tell a faithful gospel ministry from a counterfeit one? A true gospel ministry is one that seeks to see the people of God mature in Christ through the faithful proclamation of the Word. The message of the wolves infiltrating the Colossian church could never lead to maturity. That could be found only in Christ. Why shouldn't the Colossians go back to these Old Testament regulations? Because those things were merely shadows pointing ahead to the real thing, Jesus Christ. Now we live triumphantly because we've been raised with Christ!

1 & 2 Thessalonians

We often wonder about how things in life will turn out. Will our team be lifting the trophy at the end of the season? What do we do after we graduate? Will this winter ever end? What happens when we become empty nesters? But one question rises above the others: what will happen at the end of time? This world won't last forever. The Bible tells us that again and again. So what does that mean? How should we think about it?

The Thessalonian Christians were dealing with similar questions 2,000 years ago. Paul reminds them that though they were suffering, opposition to the gospel was everywhere. In fact, Paul, Silas, and Timothy were opposed even as they first brought the message of Jesus to Thessalonica! These two letters to the Thessalonians probably came only a few months apart. Paul had a shepherd's heart for these wondering sheep, that's for sure. He encouraged them to remain faithful to Jesus and be fruitful in the Holy Spirit even through trials and difficulty. The Lord was working in their lives, and God would sustain them as they waited for Christ to return.

The Lord does this for us, too. We know that Christ hasn't yet returned at the end of the age. In fact, that was one of the things the Thessalonians were struggling with. Would Christ come back for us, His people? Has He forgotten or abandoned us? Certainly not! The believers who have died will be raised in glorious, resurrection bodies. *"We who are still alive and are left will be caught up together with them in the clouds to meet the Lord in the air. And so we will be with the Lord forever"* (1 Thessalonians 4:17). What wonderful news! We are assured that though we live in a fallen world, we know what happens at the end: Jesus wins! That's why we can have confidence to live for Him in the present.

1 Timothy

Some relationships just seem to work. The people click; the timing is perfect. That's how it was for the Apostle Paul and Pastor Timothy. Paul was considerably older than Timothy, so their friendship was like the relationship between a father and son. In fact, Paul calls Timothy *"my true son in the faith"* at the beginning of this letter. It is likely that Timothy was converted to Christ under Paul's apostolic ministry.

The pair had traveled together on Paul's missionary journeys but now had been separated. When Paul departed from the city of Ephesus and went to Macedonia, he left Timothy to help the Ephesian church. Word had reached Paul's ears that there were still problems in Ephesus. He would go to them in person, but first he would write a letter of instructions to his son in the faith, the pastor of Ephesus. Paul told Timothy to oppose false teachers, do the work of a faithful pastor, lead in acceptable worship of the Lord, train up elders and deacons in the right way, and live lovingly among the brothers and sisters.

We read a lot about the church of Christ. Paul says in 3:14–15, "*Although I hope to come to you soon, I am writing you these instructions so that, if I am delayed, you will know how people ought to conduct themselves in God's household, which is the church of the living God, the pillar and foundation of the truth.*" How can the church of Christ have confidence, even in the midst of a pagan city with corruption all around? Paul's answer is straightforward: the church of Christ can have confidence because of the Christ of the church. He says in 3:16, "*He appeared in a body, was vindicated by the Spirit, was seen by angels, was preached among the nations, was believed on in the world, was taken up in glory.*"

Timothy could be confident that his work of restoring the Ephesian church could be done. And it's why we can be confident, too, as we proclaim the gospel and defend the truth from error. We are the church of Christ, and we have the Christ of the church.

2 Timothy

The Apostle Paul may be the most well-known figure in the entire Bible, other than Jesus. Paul was the man who persecuted the church before he was miraculously converted by the risen Christ Himself, the Apostle to the gentiles, the one God used to bring the gospel to Europe, and the author of 13 of the 27 New Testament books. But like all men, Paul died. Unlike most men, however, he died as a martyr because he was a believer in his Savior, Jesus Christ.

The gospel had been under attack from the beginning. Even during Christ's earthly ministry, He faced opposition. Many conspired together to kill Him. After His death, resurrection, and ascension, things didn't get any friendlier. The good news of Jesus was still rejected and opposed everywhere.

The messengers who brought this gospel were often persecuted, as well, including the high profile Apostle Paul. He was imprisoned in Rome by the time he was writing this second letter to Timothy, and he knew he wasn't getting out. Not this time. Nero was turning up the pressure on believers, and Paul would soon meet his end. So what did he do? He wrote his friend and son in the faith, Pastor Timothy.

These are the last recorded words of the Apostle Paul. As surprising as it might be to us, he was full of hope! Hope in Jesus, the Savior he knew would never abandon him, not even in death. Paul encouraged Timothy to remain faithful to Jesus and committed to the gospel of grace. Why? Because Jesus is enough. Paul's Savior had sustained him; Paul knew He would do the same for all of His people, especially when they struggle.

Believers have this sure security. Family and friends may leave, jobs may end, and banks may fail us. But Jesus never changes. He remains faithful to us, and we in turn desire to remain faithful to Him to the very end. That's why we need to not only hold onto the gospel message ourselves, but we should also defend it from anyone who would twist it. Proclaim it to others! In doing so, we're telling the great story, and it's all about Jesus!

Titus

In the book of Titus, we have another church, another pastor, and another son. As with Timothy, Paul wrote to help Titus, giving him instructions for his pastoral ministry. That's why this letter is known as one of Paul's pastoral epistles, alongside 1 and 2 Timothy.

Titus knew Paul quite well. He had accompanied Paul on his third missionary journey. Much like Timothy, Titus was left to help a church put things in order. Instead of being left at Ephesus, though, Titus was pastoring on the Mediterranean island of Crete.

Titus was to appoint elders in the different churches on the island, rebuke rebellious people, and *"teach what is in accord with sound doctrine"* (2:1). Titus, like Timothy, was a young leader in the church who may have felt overwhelmed. Paul reminded Titus the same way he did for Timothy that his confidence was in his Savior. We read in 2:11–14 that *"the grace of God that brings salvation has appeared to all men. It teaches us to say 'No' to ungodliness and worldly passions, and to live self-controlled, upright and godly lives in this present age, while we wait for the blessed hope—the glorious appearing of our great God and Savior, Jesus Christ, who gave himself for us to redeem us from all wickedness and to purify for himself a people that are his very own, eager to do what is good."*

We have the same assurance that Titus had to proclaim the gospel and defend the truth. We aren't going forward in our own strength. Christ is with us, is in us, and is coming back for us soon. You and I take 1:9 to heart; we *"hold firmly to the trustworthy message,"* the message which tells us the great story that's all about Jesus.

Philemon

The Apostle Paul wrote thirteen letters in the New Testament. Nine were written to churches, and the remaining four were sent to individuals. Of those personal letters Paul wrote, the Epistle to Philemon is unique. Timothy and Titus were pastors while Philemon had no such distinction. He was an everyday believer, a slave owner, and a friend of Paul's. The entire letter is just 25 verses long, but it packs a punch, and in a very unexpected way.

It seems that one of Philemon's slaves, a young man named Onesimus, had run away and made it to the Apostle Paul while he was in a Roman prison. Apparently Onesimus became a believer through Paul's words. There are a number of ways Paul could have responded to this unusual situation. Under the inspiration of the Holy Spirt, he addressed both slave and master as brothers in Christ. He also instructed them to treat each other as brothers, appealing to Philemon with these words: "*Perhaps the reason he was separated from you for a little while was that you might have him back for good — no longer as a slave, but better than a slave, as a dear brother. He is very dear to me but even dearer to you, both as a man and as a brother in the Lord*" (vv. 15-16).

Take note of the amazing change that the gospel of Jesus Christ creates: a Jewish Apostle, a gentile slave master, and a runaway slave all sharing equal footing before the Lord! They would receive the same salvation and would from then on treat each other as brothers. That's the difference Jesus, our Elder Brother, makes.

WEEK 50

PHILIPPIANS 1–PHILEMON

Father, You have started a good work in us and we know that You will bring it to completion. Because of Christ, You have saved us from sin and bondage. You have brought us out of a world and kingdom of darkness and into Your kingdom of grace, love, and joy. Along with Paul, we rejoice! You have saved us, not by our own striving and strength, but by the Savior. Every knee will bow and every tongue will confess the name of Jesus. Help us to kneel now, to confess now, and to proclaim His goodness everywhere we go. Let the joy in Your love to us and in our Savior Jesus be evidenced in our lives.

AMEN.

☐ *Day 344:* Philippians 1–4
☐ *Day 345:* Colossians 1–4
☐ *Day 346:* 1 Thessalonians 1–5
☐ *Day 347:* 2 Thessalonians 1–3
☐ *Day 348:* 1 Timothy 1–6
☐ *Day 349:* 2 Timothy 1–4
☐ *Day 350:* Titus 1–3; Philemon

Hebrews

A three-word summary of the book of Hebrews could be, "Jesus is better." The words of Hebrews probably originally were a sermon, though we do not know who wrote or preached them. But Jesus is better, and that's what the preacher wanted his hearers to know. Specifically, it was written to Jewish believers who were tempted to look back at the Old Testament priests, sacrifices, and temple for their salvation.

They were facing pressure, both within and without; they were in a real bind. To be a first-century Jewish believer was to be seen as a traitor, a turncoat, or someone who had turned from Yahweh, abandoned the temple, and even abandoned their blood relatives who were still practicing Jews.

They were leaving behind what was familiar and comforting, perhaps having that nagging suspicion that Jesus isn't enough.

That's why this book is so beautiful. The preacher of this sermon wants his Jewish brothers and sisters to know that we can't find anything better than Jesus. All that we read about in the Old Testament was always pointing ahead to Him in the first place. Jesus is the Word of God, the final revelation the Lord has given to His people. Jesus shines in glory above all things in creation. He's better than the angels or Moses or anyone. Jesus brings us into eternal rest, defeating all our enemies and bringing us into God's presence. He's better than Joshua; Jesus is the high priest who lives forever. He's better than the old Levitical priesthood; He's the sacrifice whose blood truly does remove our sins.

The former things were only shadows and previews. The main event is here! Don't go backwards, even if it's familiar and comforting. Don't look for another Savior or Mediator or Prophet or Sacrifice. Look for Jesus. He's more than enough for us.

James

Proof is valuable, though sometimes hard to nail down. Proof of purchase can fly away with the wind if you accidentally toss out the receipt. Proof that you scored a hole-in-one on the golf course requires other people who are with you and paying attention. But what about proof of faith in Jesus? Is there even such a thing? The Epistle of James tells us that there is, and that we can see it.

There are several men by the name of James whom we read about in the New Testament. The writer of the book of James was the half-brother of Jesus. He would have been one of the siblings who formerly declared Jesus out of His mind (see Mark 3:21). But now James identifies himself as a servant of the Lord Jesus Christ.

Persecution had arisen in Jerusalem, leading to a scattering of Jewish believers to the rest of the Mediterranean world. It's those Jewish Christians — *"the twelve tribes scattered among the nations"* (1:1) — to whom James writes this letter.

In the various places where they were dispersed, they still had one thing in common: that the Savior they trusted would impact how they lived. We see the Apostle Paul argue against people trusting in their own works. It seems James' readers had a different problem: they failed to understand how comprehensive grace really is. They thought that the gospel message meant that they didn't have to obey God. Of course, that isn't how things ought to be. Instead, our Lord enables us to live a life of grateful obedience because of the grace He has given us. You can say you believe in Christ, but James reminds us that empty talk is cheap. Indeed, *"even the demons believe that — and shudder"* (2:19).

Jesus backed up His words with His actions, and He calls us to do the same. Our good works cannot contribute a single thing to our salvation. However, they are proof that God has been at work in us. True faith leads to sincere obedience. He wants all of us. He'll keep working on us until the end.

1 Peter

When you read the four gospel books, you see that
Peter is often putting his foot in his mouth. Over
and over again Peter would say the wrong thing at
the wrong time. We all probably relate to that on
some level. Yet here he was, decades after Jesus' death
and resurrection, an apostle of Jesus Christ writing
under the inspiration of the Holy Spirit. He was not
a perfect man, but he certainly was a changed man,
changed by God Himself.

Peter wrote this letter from Rome, 30 years
or so after Jesus ascended to heaven, at about the
same time the Apostle Paul was martyred for his
proclamation of Jesus. Peter was writing to a group of
congregations in Asia Minor (what we now know as
Turkey). The Christians there were being persecuted

by the Romans — facing false accusations, unjust
suffering, and even threats.

Peter was no stranger to these things. Though
he had denied His Lord on the night of His arrest and
trial, Peter had since suffered for the sake of Christ
(see Acts 5:40; 12:1–5). How did he persevere? He
knew Who Jesus is. And he knew what Jesus had
given to him: grace, peace, and strength. By suffering
unjustly in a way that no one ever had before or since,
Jesus became the Ultimate Elect Exile who suffered
for us in our place. That's why we can live for Him,
even when we face opposition. Our Lord will never
let us go.

2 Peter

Paul's last written words were in his second letter to Timothy; Peter's last recorded words are here in 2 Peter. He probably sent this letter from Rome while the government was persecuting Christians. So what did he want his flock to know before his life would end in 65 A.D. at the hand of Emperor Nero?

Peter wanted to encourage his readers to mature in their knowledge of God's grace and to respond to it. He reminded them that we are pilgrims on this earth. This isn't our final home, so we shouldn't live like it is.

These believers were dealing with false doctrine and bad behavior in the church. Apparently, troublemakers were coming in and saying that there would be no final judgment.

Therefore, live as you please! These false teachings
were leading some believers astray.

Peter tells his gentile readers that although
they were formerly pagans, now they have the
same standing as believing Jews. Every Christian's
salvation depends on Christ's righteousness, not
our works or ethnicity. His salvation is sufficient to
cleanse us and make us new. Peter says we are already
clean in God's sight, having His power at work
within us because of Jesus.

Whom should we believe — the false
teachers and their myths, or the apostles who were
eyewitnesses? Peter reminds us that the false teachers
were denying something that they didn't know
anything about. We can know that what we have
heard about Jesus is true because it comes from God.

Peter was one of the three eyewitnesses on
the mountain of transfiguration who saw a preview
of Jesus in His glory and heard the Father's voice.
God has continued to speak in His Word. Often the
best defense against something false is knowing what
is true. Because we know the true gospel, we know
false teachers have not been sent from God.

Be assured that Jesus Christ died, is risen, is
reigning from heaven, and will come again. Believe
the gospel. Believe that Jesus is a complete Savior.

Know the red flags of false teachers. Read, hear, believe, and listen to the Word. It tells us about Christ and that He will finish the work He started.

1 John

"Says who?" We all knew a kid who loved to say these words. (Maybe we ourselves were that kid!). Some things do need to come from an authority to have any significance. Words coming from a teacher or police officer will usually carry a lot more weight than those from a child. That's especially true about eternal things. Who says this or that?

The Apostle John had a good answer. He began his first letter by telling his readers that the message he proclaimed came from Jesus Himself, the One who was from the beginning, God the Son in the flesh. The Apostle John was a witness of Jesus Christ and that was important because false teachers were claiming that they knew better. They insisted that Jesus didn't really have a physical body, that salvation wasn't actually by faith in Him. John has an answer for that: he touched Jesus! This same Christ who came in the flesh gave a message to His disciples: God is light.

When false teachers come preaching a different gospel, look at their lives. Take note that they are not walking in the light. 1 John is a book written to give believers assurance of their salvation. As John says in chapter 5, "*I write these things to you who believe in the name of the Son of God so that you may know that you have eternal life*" (v. 13). The false teachers couldn't provide that. For all their talk and pride, they couldn't give eternal life to anyone. Only Jesus can do that, and He does so through the gospel.

Let this simple summary of the Christian life sink in: believe in Jesus; love God and your brothers and sisters. Why? Because God is light, and when Jesus came, the true light came with Him. Darkness was overcome. So live like it! You're being remade into Jesus' image by God's power. Live so that people can see the family resemblance. Remember the blessings that you have in Jesus. He Himself is the One who gave the gospel to His apostles, the very same gospel that John proclaims in this letter.

WEEK 51

HEBREWS 1–1 JOHN 5

Long ago, Father, in many ways and at many times, You spoke to Your people. But now You have spoken to us fully and finally in the person and work of Jesus Christ. The sacrifices that Your people performed in the times of Israel are over. You have supplied the final sacrifice. Jesus Christ has atoned for sin once and for all. We look forward to His return, when He will come not to deal with sin but to bring us into Your presence forever. Help us to keep our eyes on Jesus, the author and finisher of our faith. Help us to enter Your rest, and to be the kind of people that follow Jesus and finish the race You set before us. We aren't strong enough to do it, but through Christ You will bring us home. In Jesus' name,

AMEN.

2 & 3 John

The Apostle John was an old man when he wrote his three letters and the Book of Revelation. All were probably written towards the end of his life, maybe even after the other apostles had died. It's striking how he changed over the years. Or more precisely, it is amazing how much work the Holy Spirit had done in his life!

Remember, John and his brother James were known as the Sons of Thunder. They wanted Jesus to call down judgment from heaven on those who had rejected Him. But now John is different. In these letters we catch a glimpse of a pastoral man, an apostle who is also like a spiritual grandfather.

John picks up in these letters where he left off in 1 John, encouraging his listeners to remain faithful to the truth about Jesus Christ. No substitute is worth it, no matter what other people might say! In 2 John he warns against showing hospitality to false teachers. It seems that people had been going around to the different churches, trying to get them to buy into a false gospel. Sounds familiar, doesn't it? John put his foot down about this. *"Many deceivers, who do not acknowledge Jesus Christ as coming in the flesh, have gone out into the world. Any such person is the deceiver and the antichrist"* (v. 7). These are harsh, but true words. Furthermore, John says believers should not welcome such people into their homes or into their pulpits. *"Anyone who welcomes them shares in their wicked work"* (v. 11). We ought to love the truth, after all, because the One who is the Way, the Truth, and the Life has given us everything we need.

In 3 John, the script is flipped. Instead of writing to believers and warning them against being hospitable to false teachers, John speaks about showing hospitality to those who truly believe in Jesus and obey His commands.

Taken together, these two letters say that we who trust in Jesus have been put together in one body, so we should seek to keep false teachers out. But also we must be hospitable to those who love the truth. After all, the God of Truth loves us!

Jude

The Epistle of Jude can be a forgotten letter, with its 25 short verses slipped in before we get to Revelation. But we must not neglect this little book which is full of gold.

We don't know much about Jude, except that he was the half-brother of Jesus and full-brother of James. Testimony from outside the Bible indicates that he was an influential figure in the early church. He urged his readers to *"contend for the faith that was once for all entrusted to the saints"* (v. 3).

But who were these people, and why was this contending so necessary? We don't know exactly who they were — other than it seems to be a church facing similar problems as the Christians to whom James wrote. False teachers had come and told these believers that God's grace in Christ meant that they could live however they wanted. So Jude told these Christians to persevere in the faith and in what the Word of God told them. To do this they needed to make sure that their lives were consistent with their faith.

We face the same sorts of challenges today. False teachers are everywhere. And our remaining sin tempts us to treat God's grace as a license to sin. We need to listen to Jude's instructions: reject false teachers and focus on Jesus. Jude ends this letter a beautiful benediction that may be familiar to you. *"To him who is able to keep you from falling and to present you before his glorious presence without fault and with great joy — to the only God our Savior be glory, majesty, power and authority, through Jesus Christ our Lord, before all ages, now and forevermore! Amen"* (vv. 24-25).

Revelation

For many Christians, the book of Revelation is the most confusing book of the Bible. Nevertheless, do not give up reading and interpreting it! In fact, Revelation itself tells us that it is profitable for us. *"Blessed is the one who reads aloud the words of this prophecy, and blessed are those who hear it and take to heart what is written in it, because the time is near"* (1:3). The message of Revelation is a triumphant one. Christ reigns and will one day return in victory. This overarching theme of Revelation is a comfort to all Christians in all times and places.

In the first chapter, we see Christ calling the Apostle John to be His prophet to the church. The letters to the seven churches are very similar to some of the words the Old Testament prophets wrote to

Israel and Judah. Throughout these letters we read, *"Whoever has ears, let them hear what the Spirit says to the churches."* So these letters were written to particular churches, but they also were written for us. We imitate the positive things and learn from the negatives.

The rest of the book (4:1–22:9) is about the victory of Christ over His enemies and the enemies of His people. It was meant to comfort its original audience — believers in the first century who were facing either pressure or outright persecution. Remember, these brothers and sisters needed to hear that God was still in charge, and that Christ would still be victorious, even when the kingdoms of the earth turn beastly.

Christ's people on earth are in a spiritual war, but He is ruling over all things now, and He will one day return to rescue His people from their enemies. John wrote this book so that Christ's people on earth would persevere in the faith and cling to their Savior who lived and died for them and is also reigning over all things.

We are living in different circumstances than the original readers of this book. We aren't experiencing persecution from the government like they were. We aren't seeing the apostles being killed off one-by-one, wondering what the future holds when Christ's special messengers are gone. But the book of Revelation should still give us confidence — Jesus reigns, and He's coming back, no matter how bleak things look.

Revelation is the last book in the great story that's all about Jesus. We know that this is how the story ends: *"Now the dwelling of God is with men, and he will live with them. They will be his people, and God himself will be with them and be their God. He will wipe every tear from their eyes. There will be no more death or mourning or crying or pain, for the old order of things has passed away"* (21:3–4).

WEEK 52

2 JOHN–REVELATION 22

Oh, Lord, as we come to the end of our journey through Your Word, we are astounded at Your marvelous mercy. You truly are the faithful God, the One who saves Your people yesterday, today, and forever. You are preparing a feast for us even now, and we pray that You will continue to strengthen us to walk with Jesus day by day. Help us to hear Your voice as we return to Your Word. Cause us to remain steadfast through suffering and trials. In the face of opposition, make us show grace and humility rather than arrogance. We long for the day when we will meet Jesus Christ face to face, and to see Him as He is. Help us look with hope. By Your Spirit, strengthen our weak hands. Let us live life captivated by Your grace. Keep us safe and bring us home. In the mighty and matchless name of Jesus,

AMEN.

☐ *Day 358:* 2 John; 3 John; Jude ☐ *Day 362:* Revelation 12–14
☐ *Day 359:* Revelation 1–3 ☐ *Day 363:* Revelation 15–17
☐ *Day 360:* Revelation 4–7 ☐ *Day 364:* Revelation 18–19
☐ *Day 361:* Revelation 8–11 ☐ *Day 365:* Revelation 20–22

Conclusion

This is not the end.

Over the past year, you have been soaking in God's Word, learning how it points to Jesus, and praying for the truth of Christ to draw you closer to Him. If you made it this far, then you already know that with every reading and meditation, the richness of God's Word begins to transform your heart and mind.

Wherever you turn next in your Christian walk, we pray this book has had a meaningful impact on the way you view Christ in all of Scripture and all of life. King David delighted in the Word of the Lord; the Apostle Paul earnestly spread the gospel message to the ends of the earth. Likewise, may you be a faithful disciple who glorifies God every day.

At the beginning of this Bible reading journey,

we reflected on how Jesus often shows up where we least expect. If you found that to be the case over the past year, we'd like to make you aware of another resource to help you draw closer to Jesus through His Word. It's called the *Psalms Reading Guide*.

The book of Psalms has some unique aspects to it, and not just because it is the book of the Bible with more chapters than any other. The poetic writing of the book of Psalms inspires readers to pray, sing, worship, and meditate on who God is and what He has done. It would be the perfect next step for you. As you reflect deeply on the Psalms, you'll see advanced echoes of Jesus on every page.

You can find Haven's *Psalms Reading Guide* by visiting our website at haventoday.org or by requesting it over the phone at (800) 654-2836.

May God's Word revealing that it is all about Jesus be ever-present in your mind and forever written on your heart.